Love Revolution

REDISCOVERING THE
LOST COMMAND
OF JESUS

GAYLORD ENNS

XULON PRESS

Scott –

Huge thanks for
your love & support
of us in this
mission and
message.

DEDICATION

Most of you will never know my dad, Herman. He comes from stoic German stock. He was one of fourteen children born to an immigrant from the Ukraine, Dietrich Enns and his wife, Sara. They had seven boys and seven girls. Dad is the oldest boy in the family.

We just celebrated his ninety-ninth birthday. He still mows his own lawn. A few weeks ago, I helped Dad repair a broken fence post in his backyard. By the time I arrived, he had already dug the posthole. That's Dad!

Vocationally, he was a dairy farmer, carpenter and building contractor. He and my (late) mother, Katie, had four children, three girls and then a boy. Mom is in heaven now, having left us just after Christmas in 1969.

When Dad married Iris in 1971, it was as if God sent us a special gift to fill a huge hole in our hearts. For thirty-seven years, Iris has been mom to us, the only grandmother our children have known.

It's to my dad that I dedicate this book.

Dear Dad,

It is an honor to dedicate this book to you. I've had the privilege of learning from many, but without question, I've learned more from you than any other person on the planet.

You are such an important part of this story. Some of my earliest memories are of the little country church we attended. You gathered us in the family room each evening to read from the Bible and to kneel in prayer together before bedtime. The values you demonstrated made an indelible impression on us.

You continue to have such a significant place in our lives. We treasure your daily prayers for us—your children, grandchildren, great-grandchildren and great great-grandchildren.

We are so glad you are still here with us. Thanks, Dad, for all your hard work and for helping to make our Christian faith a daily reality.

It is with deep gratitude that I dedicate this book to you.

I love you, Dad!

Your son,
Gaylord

March 2008

WORDS OF APPRECIATION

A thousand "thank-you's" go out with this book. So many of you have supported us in so many ways as we launched a whole new mission late in life—investing in pastors and next-generation leaders. Your friendship, giving, and prayers have been invaluable to us.

To Chico pastors, you have had a very significant role in my completing this book. Many of the thoughts in it were nurtured in the context of our fellowship. You listened to my early ideas on this topic and provided such meaningful comments. While I do not assume your agreement with all that I have written here, you have affirmed the importance of Jesus' Command. Thank you!

We have been encouraged repeatedly by a circle of close friends without which we couldn't have arrived at this day. Some of you are in Christian ministry, others in secular vocations, and still others devoted to raising a family. We owe a debt of love to each of you. Thank you so much for your help and encouragement along the way!

To my small group, you have been the friends everyone dreams of having. Our weekly time together over the last thirteen years has been used by God to make this journey possible. You have helped me process life and the ideas in this book, embracing them as a lifestyle. More than words can express, thank you for being my friends.

To our children and family, you have been an amazing source of inspiration to us. Your affirmation of this message has given us courage at very pivotal stages of writing. Your constant love is priceless. You bring us so much joy in the journey. Thank you!

Patti, you are the "wife of my youth" and you continue to grow more beautiful with time. You are a treasure to me. Thanks so much for believing in me and being such a vibrant part of my life—nearly forty years now. Your faith and partnership with me in this season of life are such of gift. I could not have come to this day without your love and hard work. Thanks, Babe!

Above all, thank you, God, for your mercies that are new every morning. Knowing you as Father, Son and Holy Spirit is a mystery beyond words and yet a reality without which I couldn't survive. Your promises and presence have made all the difference in my life. All that I am, I offer again to You as an expression of my love and worship!

CONTENTS

INTRODUCTION

François de la Rochefoucauld wrote these oft-quoted words: "The only thing constant in life is change."[1] After a few moments of thoughtful reflection, we would all nod in agreement with this seventeenth century philosopher.

Now contrast that with the words of Micah, the Judean prophet, when he wrote, "I am the LORD, I change not."[2] Micah was speaking as an oracle of God when he made this declaration in the eighth century B.C.

From between the "God who does not change" and our "life-experience of constant change" comes this book. It is born out of the "stuff of life." It comes out of pain and brokenness and yet results in peace, joy, and hope. It is rooted in the God who does not change and yet reserves the right to make profound change in the world He created.

The truth that is at the core of this book will never change. It will never change because it is founded in the nature and character of God who said, "I change not."

Love Revolution is about loss, rediscovery, and recovery. It is about coming full-circle, back to the point of origin and that one thing which will never change. It is about returning to the feet of the Master Teacher—Jesus.

Welcome to the adventure!

---

[1] Copyright ® ThinkExist 1999-2006, thinkexit.com
[2] Micah 3:6b King James Version of the Holy Bible

A WORD FROM THE AUTHOR . . .

For all of us, life happens in a context. For that reason, I have provided a prologue, a brief account of the events that transpired in my life in the six months just prior to May 1, 2002. That Wednesday was a day of startling discovery, one that has produced profound change in my life. *Love Revolution* is about that discovery.

If you enjoy a good story and want the context in which this discovery occurred, I invite you to take few minutes to read the first section, entitled "Prologue: A Day Gone Awry."

For those of you whose primary interest is rediscovering Jesus' command, I invite you to start with Chapter 1, "An Empty Table."

Finally, the message of this book is incomplete without the last two chapters. For that reason, I urge you not to put this book aside until you've read the final two chapters, "Bridge: Words I Want to Hear" and "Conclusion: Touching the Titanic."

Enjoy!

PROLOGUE: A DAY GONE AWRY

When the sun rises, signaling a new day, you never *really* know what life will look like by the day's end. For me, Sunday, October 21, 2001, started like a thousand other Sunday mornings before it. We all have our routines. As a pastor, mine was to get up at 4:30 a.m.—5:00 at the latest, then shower, shave, and dress for the Sunday services that I had been preparing for all week.

I had learned early in my pastoral ministry that it was especially important on Sunday mornings *"to give no place to the devil."*[1] Let me explain. If anything *could* go wrong, it *would* go wrong on that day. So as a young pastor, I discovered the importance of time alone in those early hours—time to focus my heart and mind for a very demanding day. Now, with thirty-four years of full time Christian ministry under my belt, getting up and out early was a well-established habit. It was just after 5:30 that morning when I quietly closed our front door and, with briefcase in hand, walked to my car.

Our city of under 100,000 people had two places you could count on to be open that early. Denny's diner had been my Sunday morning quiet spot for years. Many times, the waitress had already spotted me driving up to the near-empty restaurant and had turned in my order. By the time I got my Bible and sermon notes positioned on the table, water and extra napkins had been delivered to the quiet corner booth.

---

[1] See Ephesians 4:27

But on this October morning, something pulled me off course. I wasn't driving down the freeway to the off-ramp that would take me to my familiar corner booth at Denny's. Rather, I was driving aimlessly down empty streets towards downtown, parking at the curb in front of a small donut shop.

By the time I stepped up to the glass display a second time and pointed to another donut, it was beginning to dawn on me that something was very different—wrong. I wrestled momentarily with a silent question, "Do you have to pay for refills here?" With my thumbnail, I was subconsciously pressing little groves into the rim of the Styrofoam cup in my hand.

As I sat alone at that unfamiliar table, I knew something wasn't working. Something was broken. I needed help. I couldn't be with people this morning. The thought of speaking at two Sunday morning services loomed in front of me like impassable canyons.

I stepped out on the sidewalk, cell phone in hand, and called my twenty-seven year old son and associate pastor. It was 5:50 a.m. I got Eric's answering machine. I left a brief message asking that he call me and quickly dialed the number of another pastor friend. I remembered that he had once volunteered, "If you ever need help, call me!"

"Thank God for friends like him," I thought as the phone rang. A quiet, sleepy voice on the other end of the line said, "Hello." It was my friend's wife. I identified myself and offered a word of apology. "I'm not doing well this morning. I need some help and I'm calling to see if Tom could speak for me today."

"He would do anything to help you, but he's not here. He's speaking at a retreat this weekend."

Just my luck. I'd never had to take someone up on this kind of offer before, and the first time I really needed help, they weren't available. I felt numb standing in the middle of the sidewalk in the early morning air. What should I do next?

Mercifully, my cell phone rang, interrupting my question. It was my son. "Hey Dad. We unplugged our phone last night so I didn't get your call 'til just now."

"Son, I . . . I'm not doing well. I'm not making it today. Could you speak for me?"

There was a brief moment of silence. "No worries, Dad. No worries."

I'll never forget those two little words—"*No worries.*" They were my introduction to a much deeper brokenness than I could imagine, but more than that, they were the first drops of soothing oil that I needed to repair my broken emotional condition. Those two words were the beginning of a yearlong sabbatical—a season of healing that would bring a most powerful explosion of truth and change my life forever.

How Deep is this Hole?

I hope you never have to experience what I am about to describe. When you plunge over the edge into severe burnout or a breakdown, you can't help wondering, "How deep is this hole? How far will I fall? When I hit bottom, what will the bottom look like? Will I ever have the strength to climb out?"

This day hadn't come without warning. I had not been sleeping well for six months. I was starting to stutter when I spoke. Decisions were getting harder to make. Increasingly, I had been experiencing depression, but not the kind that people in my congregation could see. It was the kind that settled over me like a layer of fog at the end of a long and exhausting day. But this was a day like no other—a day gone awry.

My staff and the elders of our congregation lifted all responsibilities off me and released me into a sabbatical season to facilitate my recovery. I slept for a month and a half. I don't mean that I slept twenty-four hours a day. I just generally slept in the morning, afternoon and night. I had no idea that anyone could be that tired, drained, depleted. I didn't—couldn't—read any books. A couple of times, I started to watch a program on TV, but after a few minutes, I would lose focus and then interest. "Why would *anyone ever* want to watch this?"

What I could do was watch CNN. Actually, it wasn't so much watching as it was having the drone of anonymous voices in the background. It actually helped me do what I wanted to do most . . . *sleep*!

It was hardest on my wife, Patti. I remember one day about three weeks into my breakdown. I had just finished eating the sandwich she had fixed me for lunch. I was lying back down on the couch when I saw her standing over me.

"Honey, you're scaring me! You slept all night. You napped all morning. If you sleep this afternoon, aren't you afraid you won't be able to sleep tonight?"

"Babe, I can hardly wait until tonight so I can go to bed!"

After a month of this had gone by, I started to get worried. I couldn't shake the thought, "I think I'm turning into a slug!"

How long was this extreme fatigue going to last? I was already under my doctor's care and was taking the antidepressant that he had prescribed several months earlier. Following my burnout/breakdown, our church elders asked me to see a Christian counselor. The two hours I had each week with this trusted professional provided a wonderful oasis for me. It was a place to process and gain much needed understanding of the issues that contributed to my descent into this broken state.

My persistent fatigue was disturbing to both of us. We sought additional counsel to soothe our troubled minds. I was told, "Trust your body. When your body has had the rest it needs, it will tell you." And sure enough, after six weeks of mostly sleep, natural energy started to return—very slowly. I didn't want to sleep *all* day *and* all night.

As Christmas approached, one of the first small tasks I tackled was putting up the outdoor lights on our home. In years past, putting up the lights had always been an unwelcome intrusion into my busy schedule. It involved finding *which* of the large plastic storage boxes in the garage marked "Christmas Decorations" actually *had* the lights in it. After clearing that hurdle, there was untangling the strands and then stringing them around the eaves while balancing on a ladder that seemed to constantly shift in the rain soaked flowerbeds. Then came the magical moment when I plugged them in and stepped back to see . . . that two of the six strands remained unlit, like a big mocking grin with a couple of missing teeth. Ugh!

This time, I had all day. I plugged in each strand *before* stringing them, separating them into those that worked and those that needed repair. Then I patiently and deliberately worked over the strands that were defective, examining each bulb until I found the faulty one and replaced it.

When I stepped back this year to look at the Christmas "stars" that outlined the front of our home, I had a small sense of the Creator's joy. "And God saw that it was good."

It seemed that it had been a long time since I had experienced that sense of satisfaction about anything, especially Christmas lights! But by far, the best was yet to come. God was repairing the "burned out bulbs" in my life. And when the "lights" would come back on for me, my spiritual worldview would be changed dramatically. But first, there was one more surprise.

A Surprise at the Bottom

For the first time, I was facing the fact that I was the steward of something more than my spiritual wellbeing. I had a soul that needed care and a body that I could no longer neglect, even for a cause as lofty as pastoral ministry. My annual physical examination had been scheduled well before my breakdown and by the time it rolled around in December, I was taking a more proactive approach to my overall health.

My doctor had just finished the exam. He was sitting at a small table near me writing some notes in my chart. I was buttoning my shirt.

"Doc, should I be getting one of those "colon things?"

Without looking up, he asked, "How old are you?"

"Fifty-six."

He continued to write, only now on his prescription pad. Yes, his office would schedule the colonoscopy and they would call me with the date and time.

They scheduled the procedure for two months later. That left Patti and me free to enjoy our first Christmas ever without the extra planning and activities pastors experience during this season. More importantly, it left me free to continue the healing process.

The middle of January brought a significant milestone in my healing and recovery. As I was showering one morning, I had my first creative thought in months. It was wonderful. Minutes later as I stood drying off, the excitement of having my first creative thought was not diminished by the fact that, for the life of me, I could not remember *what* that creative thought had been. Just knowing that I had *had one* was enough for that day!

Early March rolled around. My colonoscopy was uneventful except for one small polyp the doctor discovered and summarily removed. The next day, Patti and I drove to southern California for the weekend. Thoughts of the procedure were forgotten as we enjoyed time together with our daughter, Erin, and her husband near the beach in Santa Monica. I didn't give any more thought to it until the weekend was over and we were winding our way back home. We had just passed over the Grapevine when my wife reminded me that I should call my doctor to get the results of the biopsy.

I dialed the number of my doctor's office. His front desk put me through to him. I identified myself and we exchanged greetings. "I'm calling to get the results of my test from last week."

"Where are you calling from?"

"My wife and I are driving up I-5. Just came over the Grapevine. We've been in LA visiting family."

"Are you on a cell phone?"

"Yes."

"Possibly it would be better if you would call me when you get back to Chico."

"Actually, it's fine to talk now. Very little traffic on I-5 today."

"Are you by yourself?"

"No. My wife is right here with me in the car." I was starting to feel slightly irritated. It was as if he wasn't really *listening* to me.

"Would you like to pull over?"

At that moment, it dawned on me that the doctor had something to say that he wasn't sure I was ready to hear. It had never occurred to me that the colonoscopy was anything more than a routine procedure that I had spontaneously requested.

"Doctor, I live with a lot of peace. Whatever you have to tell me, you can say it now."

"The biopsy showed some cells with *marked dysphasia*. We will need to do some follow-up surgery. I have two surgeons that I would like to recommend to you."

It was obvious to me that *marked dysphasia* were "code words" used in my case to keep me from understanding what he was really saying.

"Doctor, does this have anything to do with cancer?"

"Why don't you call me tomorrow when you get back in town."

The next day found me sitting in his office. As he looked across his desk at me, he broke the news. It was cancer. They hadn't been able to find a margin of clear tissue around the polyp that he had removed.

"Don't be mad at me if we don't find more cancer, but I can't sleep without knowing if we got it all. If you were eighty-five I wouldn't worry about it, but at your age, I can't risk the possibility."

A week later, they had taken out a foot and a half of my colon along with the lymphatic systems that were associated with that section. The good news was that they found no more cancer, the best possible outcome in these circumstances.

My recovery from this major surgery took the balance of March and all of April. That brought me to the month of May and a day that would revolutionize my understanding of the Christian faith—what it meant to be a follower and learner of Jesus.

CHAPTER 1

AN EMPTY TABLE

May 1, 2002, is a day I will never forget. I awakened that Wednesday morning with a very clear thought: "I'm ready to study the Bible!"

The excitement I felt was only heightened by the fact that I hadn't studied the Bible or prepared a sermon for months. Six months earlier, I had been a successful pastor on my way to speak at multiple Sunday morning worship services. But after nearly three and a half decades of serving others, I had lost my grip and gone spiraling over the edge into the depths of a breakdown.

For the first six weeks after my crash, I slept most of the time. I had no interest in reading a book or watching TV. During the first three months, I couldn't read anything, not even my familiar Bible.

As a pastor with a teaching gift, studying the Scriptures had been such a life-giving part of who I was. I can only try to communicate to you what it felt like to make such a joyful declaration! I was back, excited to be awake after a long, long night.

As I settled in at our kitchen table to study the Bible, I had the sense that I was sitting down at a large empty table, one that had once been filled with many important tasks. Now that table had been tipped over. Everything that had filled my life had slid off and now it was an empty space with only one thing, my Bible, in front of me.

I *was* ready to study the Bible. But *where* would I start? I don't know if you can appreciate what I was experiencing in that moment, but the Bible, with over a thousand pages in it, is a big book! Should I start in Genesis, Psalms, one of the Gospels, Revelation? I needed a place, a topic, or a point of focus to actually do what I was ready to do that day.

It was in that moment that the Great Commission came to my mind. I opened my laptop computer Bible to Matthew 28:18 and started to read these familiar words.

> All authority in heaven and on earth has been given to me. Therefore go and make disciples of all nations, baptizing them in the name of the Father and of the Son and of the Holy Spirit, and teaching them to obey everything I have commanded you. And surely I am with you always, to the very end of the age.[1]

There was a comforting, almost *warming*, sense that went through me as my eyes focused on the familiar words displayed on the screen in front of me. These words were literally the reason I had become who I was. I had ministered to people on the authority of the Great Commission for thirty-five years. This passage had been the theme of some of my most passionate sermons and teachings throughout those decades of Christian ministry.

Quickly, my attention shifted to the other half of the split screen on my laptop. Apparently, when I was preparing my last sermon six months earlier, I had been referencing a Bible text in Robert Young's *Literal Translation of the Bible*.

> 'Given to me was all authority in heaven and on earth;
> having gone, then, disciple all the nations, (baptizing

---

[1] Matthew 28:18-20

them - to the name of the Father, and of the Son, and of the Holy Spirit, teaching them to observe all, whatever I did command you,) and lo, I am with you all the days - till the full end of the age.'[1]

Immediately I was struck with Young's use of the parentheses in his translation. It was apparent that he chose to use the parenthetical enclosure because he thought it brought clarity to the instruction Jesus was giving. From my understanding of Young's translation, I paraphrased what Jesus was saying like this:

I have been given all authority in heaven and on earth. Wherever you go, *make disciples of all the nations,* and know this; I am with you every day until the very end. (*By the way,* if you need to be reminded of what "making disciples" is all about, I'm embedding a two-part definition for you: [1] baptizing them in the name of the Father, and of the Son, and of the Holy Spirit, and [2] teaching them to obey all that I commanded you.)

What I was about to discover would revolutionize my understanding of the Great Commission. Young viewed the parenthetical phrase as Jesus' own embedded definition of "disciple making." In other words, he believed that Jesus was not just telling them *what to do*—disciple the nations— but also *how to do it.* Moreover, under *how to do it,* Jesus had introduced two distinct halves of disciple making, (1) *baptizing them* and (2) *teaching them.*

If my brain had been wired to an excitement meter in that moment, it would have registered off the scale. For the first time, I was considering the possibility that Jesus had actually

---

[1] Matthew 28:18b-20 Robert Young, *Young's Literal Translation of the Old and New Testaments,* 1898

embedded his own definition of disciple making in the Great Commission, a definition that contained two parts.

The first part—*baptizing them*—seemed to be tied directly to *faith in Jesus Christ*. Believing in Him was the initiating step in discipleship and led to baptism, a formal declaration of one's faith in Jesus. For the new believer, baptism was a point of identification as one of Jesus' disciples and a member of His New Covenant family.

The second part—*teaching them*—was the process of communicating to those newly initiated believers everything Jesus had commanded His original disciples. Frankly, it had never seemed as clear or as simple to me as it did in that moment. Imagine the excitement that reverberated in me as these simple insights dawned on a mind that had been "flat lined" for months!

I had done a fair amount of evangelism over the years. I had shared the Good News with many people and watched as they put their faith in Jesus. During decades of pastoral ministry, I had baptized many people. I felt that I had a good understanding of the "baptizing them" half of discipleship.

For some reason, the "teaching them" half gripped me in that moment. *What all had Jesus commanded His disciples to obey?* In that moment, I knew that I had to find the answer to that question. That would be the focus of my first Bible study.

Little did I know that before that day was over, I would be shaken with a profound new realization, one that would lead me to ask another question. These two questions, when answered, would change my understanding of disciple-making forever.

An amazing journey had just begun.

CHAPTER 2

ALL THAT I COMMANDED

My study would focus on finding the answer to the question "What all *did* Jesus command His disciples to obey?" My goal would be to find the ten, twenty, forty, or more things that Jesus had *commanded*. Then I would systematize them into a logical format, one I could use to teach new Christians.

Because Jesus had said, "teaching them to obey everything I have *commanded* you,"[1] I would start my study with the obvious—the word *command* as found right there in the Great Commission. In the Greek language, the word *commanded* is *entellomai*. I typed this word and a closely related *entole* into my computer and pressed the enter key. In an instant, the eighty-seven times they were used in the New Testament flashed across the screen. I quickly printed out the verses that contained either of these two words.

As I started to read the verses, I found fifteen times when this word *command* was used to direct someone, or a small group of people, to take some immediate action. Because it was an action uniquely commanded them at that time, there was no ongoing application for us today. For example, Jesus used this word *command* to prohibit Peter, James and John from prematurely telling others what they had seen when He was transfigured before them on the mountain.

---

[1] Matthew 28:20b

> As they were coming down from the mountain, Jesus *commanded (entellomai)* them, saying, "Tell the vision to no one until the Son of Man has risen from the dead."[1]

I found a second way the word *command* was used. There were nearly forty times in the New Testament when it was used in reference to the *commandments* found in the Law of Moses. For example, Jesus said the following in answer to a question.

> You know the *commandments [entole]*: 'Do not murder, do not commit adultery, do not steal, do not give false testimony, do not defraud, honor your father and mother.'[2]

However, it was the third way that the word *command* was used that surprised me and gripped my attention. I found the word *command* used in the company of the word *love* over thirty times! As you read the mosaic that follows, you will get a sense of the startling connection between these two words—***command*** and ***love***. While it may seem a bit long or even repetitive, every sentence is unique. You might even try reading it aloud just to hear the words.

> *"A new **command** I give you: **Love** one another. As I have **loved** you, so you must **love** one another. By this all men will know that you are my disciples, if you **love** one another." "If you **love** me, you will obey what I **command**." "Whoever has my **commands**[3] and obeys them, he is the one who **loves** me. He who **loves** me will be **loved** by my Father, and I too will **love** him and show myself to him." "the world must learn that I **love** the Father and that I do exactly what my Father has*

---

[1] Matthew 17:9 New American Standard
[2] Mark 10:19
[3] For commentary on the mixed use of plural "commands" and singular "command," see Appendix A.

commanded me."

*"If you obey my **commands**, you will remain in my **love**, just as I have obeyed my Father's **commands** and remain in his **love**." "My **command** is this: **Love** each other as I have **loved** you. Greater **love** has no one than this, that he lay down his life for his friends. You are my friends if you do what I **command**." "This is my **command**: **Love** each other."*

*"The **commandments**, 'Do not commit adultery,' 'Do not murder,' 'Do not steal,' 'Do not covet,' and whatever other **commandment** there may be, are summed up in this one rule: '**Love** your neighbor as yourself'. **Love** does no harm to its neighbor. Therefore **love** is the fulfillment of the law."*

*"we . . . receive from him [God] anything we ask, because we obey his **commands** and do what pleases him. And this is his **command**: to believe in the name of his Son, Jesus Christ, and to **love** one another as he **commanded** us. Those who obey his **commands** live in him, and he in them."*

*"We **love** because he first **loved** us. If anyone says, 'I **love** God,' yet hates his brother, he is a liar. For anyone who does not **love** his brother, whom he has seen, cannot **love** God, whom he has not seen. And he has given us this **command**: Whoever **loves** God must also **love** his brother."*

*"This is how we know that we **love** the children of God: by **loving** God and carrying out his **commands**. This is **love** for God: to obey his **commands**. And his **commands** are not burdensome . . . ." "I am not writing you a new **command** but one we have had from*

*the beginning. I ask that we **love** one another. And this is **love**: that we walk in obedience to his **commands**. As you have heard from the beginning, his **command** is that you walk in **love**."[1]*

For the first time, I saw the striking correlation between the words *command* and *love* in the New Testament. More importantly, I saw that this correlation had its origin in the New Command that Jesus had given His disciples! This connection between the words *command* and *love* was not just an important theme that Peter, James, John, or Paul had introduced in their writings. Rather, loving one another, as they taught it, was rooted in nothing less than the New Command that Jesus gave to His disciples!

A **new command** I give you: **Love one another**. As I have loved you, so you must **love one another**. By this all men will know that you are my disciples, if you **love one another**.[2]

On that pivotal evening, Jesus did more than introduce it as a new command. He took ownership of it, calling it "my command" as He repeated it two more times before the night was over.

My command is this: Love each other as I have loved you.[3]

This is **my command**: Love each other.[4]

---

[1] John 13:34-35, 14:15, 21, 31, 15:10, 12, 14, 17, Romans 13:9-10, 1 John 3:21-24, 1 John 4:19-21, 5:2 - 4, 2 John 1:5-6
[2] John 13:34-35
[3] John 15:12
[4] John 15:17

Immediately, I was confronted with (and it seemed like for the first time) **Jesus' Commandment**. This was more than another teaching. It had the full weight of the word *command* as used in the Ten Commandments found in the Law of Moses.

And for the first time, I found myself considering the possibility that Jesus may have given us only *one command* and I had missed it! How could I have missed something so obvious?

For one thing, I had not really taken the word *command* to mean what it said. For example, when I read the Great Commission, it went like this in my mind:

"teaching them to obey everything I have *taught* you."

Yet if words mean anything (and they do), I couldn't arbitrarily substitute the word *taught* for the word *command*. Now I was confronting the possibility that while Jesus had *taught* us many things, all of which are very important, He may have *commanded* us only *one* thing, to love one another as He had loved us.

As I looked at all of the times He used the word *command*[1] in the Gospels, I discovered that Jesus applied this word uniquely to His own sayings on only two occasions. The first was in His final message to His disciples at the Last Supper. The second was in His final commission to His disciples just before His ascension.

Two points stood out to me. First, both of these unique instances came after His announcement of the New Covenant. Second, both of these unique instances were recorded by the two Gospel

---

[1] For more on the use of "command" (entellomai and entole) in the Gospels, see Appendix B.

writers who were actually present when Jesus gave His New Command—Matthew and John.[1]

Of the two unique occasions when Jesus used the word *command*, the first is in His final message when He gave the New Command to the disciples.

> A new *command* I give you: Love one another. As I have loved you, so you must love one another.[2]

The second is when He gave the Great Commission.

> Therefore go and make disciples of all nations, baptizing them in the name of the Father and of the Son and of the Holy Spirit, and teaching them to obey everything I have *commanded* you.[3]

Now I had to consider the possibility that Jesus may have used the word *commanded* in the Great Commission to highlight the significance of what He had said only weeks earlier when He introduced the New Commandment at the Last Supper. It seemed reasonable to me that Jesus, in commissioning His followers to make disciples of all the nations, would have reiterated the importance of loving one another as He had loved them. After all, their *love for one another* would be the mark of authenticity by which those who were Jesus' followers and learners would forever be identified as His disciples!

Actually, I seemed to be more familiar with the Ten Commandments that God gave through Moses than I was with

---

[1] Whereas Matthew and John were among the twelve, Mark and Luke were not. Many believe Mark was mentored by the apostle Peter and Luke by the apostle Paul.
[2] John 13:34
[3] Matthew 28:19-20a

the One Commandment[1] that God gave through Jesus Christ, His Son. How could this be? I had attended church all my life. In my training, in years of personal study, and in decades of teaching others, I could not remember being taught or teaching others that "to love one another" was Jesus' Command—the one command He owned as "His." How could I possibly have missed something so clear, so obvious, and so simple?

I had started my study that morning with a question: What all *did* Jesus command His disciples to obey? That question had led me to discover a stunning omission in my thinking. It was the *New Commandment—His Command.*

> My command is this: Love each other as I have loved you.[2]

While I may have missed the significance of the New Commandment Jesus had given, I was certain the early church fathers had not overlooked His Command. I was sure they would have much to say about something that was this important. It was to them that I would look next.

---

[1] Just as the words *Ten Commandments* given through Moses are capitalized, I have chosen to capitalize the words *One Commandment* given by Jesus.
[2] John 15:12

CHAPTER 3

THE EARLY FATHERS

The leaders of the church after the death of the twelve apostles became known as the *early fathers*. They were the overseers of a rapidly growing number of Christians between the years 100 to 325 A.D. They are also known as the ante Nicene fathers. We are given a window into their thinking through 10,000 pages of their writings.

From my perspective, these men lived as close as you could get to authentic Christian faith and practice—at least after the death of the first Apostles. That's why I was so eager to see what these fifty or so early leaders had to say about the Command that had gripped my attention. And I knew just where to look to find out what they had to say about it—Bercot's *A Dictionary of Early Christian Beliefs*.[1]

I stumbled onto David Bercot's dictionary a couple of months earlier as I was looking through the religious book section at Barnes & Noble. It was billed as *A Reference Guide to More Than 700 Topics Discussed by the Early Church Fathers*. Bercot had combed through the ten thousand pages they had written and catalogued the contents under seven hundred topics. With that many topics listed, I was sure I would "strike gold" when I looked up something as significant as Jesus' Commandment or the Command of Christ.

I got up from the kitchen table to retrieve it from a tall stack of books that had accumulated on my desk over the past six

---

[1] David W. Bercot, Editor, *A Dictionary of Early Christian Beliefs*, Peabody, Massachusetts, Hendrickson, 1998

months. As I settled back down at the kitchen table, I began to thumb through it, looking for the Command of Christ. I found CLERGY, CLOTHING, COMMUNION, CONCEPTION, but nothing on the COMMAND of Christ or CHRIST – Commandment.

Maybe it's under LAW of Christ, I thought. There was LAW of Moses, Natural LAW, Roman LAW, LAWSUITS, but no LAW of Christ.

What about just plain LOVE or CHARITY? I thought to myself. It did reference Jesus' teaching about "*loving our enemies,*" but I could find no reference to Jesus' Commandment *to love one another as He had loved us!* I was stunned. I had been so sure I would find a treasure-trove of insights and applications relating to Jesus' Command from the writings of these early church leaders. But nothing?[1]

A wave of disbelief swept over me. I had started the day with a question: *What all did Jesus command His disciples to obey?* That question had brought me to a profound personal discovery. Now I was left with a second large question: *Whatever happened to Jesus' Commandment?*

I had nowhere to go but back to the words that Jesus had spoken, "teaching them to obey everything I have commanded you."[2]

I carefully examined each word in His statement. The word *obey* caught my attention. Some Bible translations render it *observe*—"teaching them to *observe* all that *I* commanded you."[3] I actually like the word *obey* better. *Observe* is a word that on the surface seemed too casual for my taste. But in the

---

[1] See Appendix C
[2] Matthew 28:20a
[3] Matthew 28:20a KJV

Greek language, it is *tereo*, a very powerful word that means "to guard (from loss . . . by keeping the eye upon)."[1] There is nothing casual or passive about *tereo*. It is a word that implies focus, protection, and vigilance.

Suddenly, some pieces started to come together in my thinking. Jesus was saying that a central part of His assignment to His followers was to teach others *to guard—to protect from loss by never taking their eyes off*—what He had *commanded* them. Certainly that included the *New Command—His Command*—He had so recently given them.

> A new command I give you: Love one another. As I have loved you, so you must love one another.[2]

> My command is this: Love each other as I have loved you.[3]

> This is my command: Love each other.[4]

Why do we guard something? Why did Jesus tell them to guard—to protect from loss by never taking their eyes off— what He had commanded them? Because it is valuable, essential, one of a kind, and irreplaceable. Its loss would be *catastrophic!*

A better translation of Jesus' words of commission might be this:

> *teaching them to guard—to protect by never taking their eyes off—the whole of that which I commanded*

---

[1] James Strong, *The New Strong's Exhaustive Concordance of the Bible.*
[2] John 13:34
[3] John 15:12
[4] John 15:17

you.[1]

I was beginning to hypothesize why Bercot had cited no reference to Jesus' Command in the writings of the early church fathers. First, the early fathers said so little about Jesus' Commandment that it failed to flag Bercot's attention. Second, the New Command has been so obscure in our contemporary theology that Bercot didn't think of it as one of the seven hundred topics to research.

The focus of these early fathers seems to have been drawn away from the Command by the speculative ideas and doctrines that were being promoted by unscrupulous pretenders, well-meaning believers, and would-be leaders. Which of these ideas and doctrines were true, which were false, and which were heresies? They had no choice but to find answers to these questions. It was a large and unenviable challenge that these early leaders of the church could not escape. They had to preserve *orthodoxy* (right belief about God) and *orthopraxy* (right practice of the newly founded Christian faith).

To find answers and to resolve these issues, these early leaders began to communicate with one another by letter. Then they met in councils to discuss these matters and agree on right doctrine and corrective measures. Finally, they started to write creeds to ensure that the faithful would have a correct understanding of God and sound Christian doctrine.

Sadly, in the quest for orthodoxy, the New Command, to love one another as Jesus had loved us, seemed to have slipped unnoticed out of their sight. Their focus had been shifted to the speculative issues that were demanding their attention. The need to establish correct doctrine for the Christian faith had drawn their eyes off the Commandment that Jesus had told them to guard—to protect by never letting it out of their sight.

---

[1] My paraphrase of Matthew 28:20a

These early Christians had a treasure, the Command they had been given by Jesus. They loved each other deeply. This love was clearly seen in the Scriptural record of those early years.

> All the believers were together and had everything in common. Selling their possessions and goods, they gave to anyone as he had need. Every day they continued to meet together in the temple courts. They broke bread in their homes and ate together with glad and sincere hearts, praising God and enjoying the favor of all the people. And the Lord added to their number daily those who were being saved.[1]

However, with the passage of time, their love for one another was tested. Over the decades that followed, it appears that their attention drifted from the Command Jesus had given them.[2]

Beyond that, it was as if a master thief was lurking in the shadows. He had spotted the treasure. It was not that he had any use for it; actually, he hated it. If only he could steal their "mark of authenticity!" All he needed was for them to take their eyes off the Command so he could slip it from the table and into the shadows.

It seems that this thief was willing to let them have orthodoxy, but only if defined *without* the One Commandment Jesus had given them. Let them debate their doctrines, disagree with one another, even ignore and dislike each other. He would keep them so preoccupied in their quest for sound doctrine that they wouldn't even miss the stolen treasure. His wildest dream was that they would come to hate each other—better yet, kill one another—in their quest to preserve an incomplete orthodoxy!

---

[1] Acts 2:44-47
[2] Revelation 2:4-5

A core commandment of authentic Christian discipleship was fading from their vision. The unfortunate irony is that the goal of orthodoxy was to keep Christianity authentic. Yet the very mark of authenticity that Jesus had given them was being lost even as they pursued this noble goal.

It was now late afternoon May 1, 2002. After the debilitating crisis I had experienced, it was great to have recovered enough to study the Bible again. But I felt like someone *really big* had taken me by the ankles, turned me upside down, and shaken a lot of personal "theological change" out of my pockets.

I had started the day with a question: "What all *did* Jesus command His disciples to obey?" I had been confronted with a stunning omission in my thinking. While Jesus had taught us many things, He had clearly commanded us *one thing*. It was the New Commandment—His Command.

> My command is this: Love each other as I have loved you.[1]

I could no longer overlook Jesus' Commandment. In fact, it seemed impossible to overestimate its value or overemphasize its significance. It had to be a *core commandment* of authentic Christianity.

An amazing adventure was only beginning. I had no idea how profoundly this understanding would transform my daily journey of Christian faith and practice. Like the discovery of a missing piece in a puzzle, my personal discovery of Jesus' Commandment began to make the picture complete for me. When this piece was put into place, I was able to see how clearly it fit with another core commandment of authentic Christianity, one that faired much better over the centuries than the Command that Jesus had given us.

---

[1] John 15:12

It was on these two core commandments that I would focus next.

CHAPTER 4

TWO CORE COMMANDMENTS

I was amazed to discover how clearly Jesus' Commandment was connected with another well-known tenant of Christianity— God's command that we "believe in Jesus Christ." Together, these two commandments were emerging in my thinking as *the core commandments* of authentic Christianity. This new understanding was powerfully reinforced in my mind by the words of John the apostle in his first letter.

> This is his [God's] commandment, that we [1] believe in the name of His Son Jesus Christ, and [2] love one another, just as he [Jesus] commanded us.[1]

When I looked more closely at this statement, it became clear that God, seen here as Father, commanded that we "believe in the name of his Son, Jesus Christ." This was God's command to us. It was the first core commandment of Christianity. Then Jesus Christ, God's Son, commanded us "to love one another." This was the second core commandment of Christianity. John intentionally linked these two commands. Together, they were the *two core commandments* of authentic Christian discipleship.

While these two core commandments were new to me, it quickly became apparent that they weren't new to the writers of the New Testament. Consider the following quotes from the letters.

---

[1] 1 John 3:23 New American Standard

Letter to the Colossians

We always thank God, the Father of our Lord Jesus Christ, when we pray for you, because we have heard of [1][1] your faith in Christ Jesus and [2] of the love you have for all the saints[2]

Letter to the Ephesians

For this reason, ever since I heard about [1] your faith in the Lord Jesus and [2] your love for all the saints, I have not stopped giving thanks for you, remembering you in my prayers.[3]

Letter to Philemon

I always thank my God as I remember you in my prayers, because I heard about [1] your faith in the Lord Jesus and [2] your love for all the saints.[4]

Letter to the Galatians

For in Christ Jesus neither circumcision nor uncircumcision has any value. The only thing that counts is [1] faith expressing itself [2] through love.[5]

Letter to the Hebrews

let us draw near with a true heart in full assurance of [1] faith . . . (and) let us consider one another in order to stir up [2] love and good works[6]

One of the most insightful uses of the two core commands was found in the story of Paul and his friends in the city of Thessalonica.

---

[1] Brackets and enclosed numbers are mine throughout
[2] Colossians 1:3-4
[3] Ephesians 1:15-16
[4] Philemon 1:4-5
[5] Galatians 5:6
[6] Hebrews 10:22a, 24 NKJV

In short, the story[1] goes like this. Paul, Silas, and Timothy were on their second missionary journey when they arrived at Thessalonica. Paul went to the local synagogue where, for three Sabbaths in a row, he taught that Jesus was the promised Messiah, that He was crucified and raised from the dead. A significant number of people believed what he was teaching. Then trouble broke out and their host was arrested. That night, Paul and his company were smuggled out of the city and made a hasty getaway under the cover of darkness.

Apparently, Paul could not get these newly found friends, now believers in Jesus Christ, off his mind in the months that followed. He decided to send Timothy to visit them and bring back word about how they were doing. Upon Timothy's return, Paul writes his first letter to them. In it, he explains that he missed them so much that he had sent Timothy on the long journey to find out how they were doing.

> But Timothy has just now come to us from you and has brought good news about your [1] faith and [2] love.[2]

Why "good news about your *faith* and *love*?" My original thinking was that Paul was commending their *faith in God* and *love for God*. However, my understanding was amended when I continued to read his second letter to them, written only months later. As he opens his second letter, he writes the following:

> We ought always to thank God for you . . . because [1] your faith is growing more and more, and [2] the love every one of you *has for each other* is increasing.[3]

---

[1] See Acts 17:1-9

[2] 1 Thessalonians 3:6a

[3] 2 Thessalonians 1:3

It was becoming clear to me that (1) faith in Jesus Christ and (2) love for one another were indeed recognized by the writers of New Testament as marks of authenticity. Whenever they found these two expressions of grace in people, they took them to be signs of the new life that was promised to those that would put their faith in Jesus Christ.

Good News – Bad News

I was now confronted with a very real "good news – bad news" scenario. The "good news" was this: the *first core commandment*—God's command that we believe in His Son, Jesus Christ—has been taught as a central truth for much of Christian history.

The "bad news" was that while early Christians loved one another deeply, history revealed the astonishing and early loss of the *second core commandment*—Jesus' Command that we love one another as He had loved us.

Written references to Jesus' Command were rare between the years 125 – 325 A.D. Out of fifty early church fathers whose writings remain, I found only two that made direct reference to it, Clement of Alexandria and Cyprian of Carthage. Clement made one direct reference to the Command and Cyprian of Carthage made four direct references to it.

Here is one of Cyprian's four references:

> Discord cannot attain to the kingdom of heaven; to the rewards of Christ, who said, "This is my commandment that ye love one another even as I have loved you:" he cannot attain who has violated the love of Christ by

faithless dissension. He who has not charity has not God.[1]

In another treatise, Cyprian wrote these words.

But what did the Lord more frequently instill into His disciples, what did He more charge to be guarded and observed among His saving counsels and heavenly precepts, than that with the same love wherewith He Himself loved the disciples, we also should love one another?[2]

Beginning in the second century, creeds, catechisms, and formal confessions of faith became increasingly important in teaching the doctrines of Christianity. Some of the more well-known ones include the Apostles' Creed (third century), the Nicene Creed (325), the Heidelberg Catechism (1563), and the Westminster Confession of Faith (1646). Unfortunately, none of these contains a reference to Jesus' Command to love one another. In fact, the words "love one another" seem strangely absent from all of these creeds and confessions. Emphasis was increasingly placed on the Old Testament Commandments. In large part, Jesus' Command disappeared from Christian teaching. *For all practical purposes, it was lost!*

As I pondered my personal discovery of Jesus' Command, it was clear that I had a lot to learn. I did see that it was clearly linked with God's Command that we believe in His Son, Jesus Christ. For the first time, I was seeing faith in Jesus Christ and love for one another as the *core commandments* of historic

---

[1] Cyprian, *On the Unity of the Church*, The Ante-Nicene Fathers, Vol 5, AGES, Edited By A. Roberts And J Donaldson, p. 874

[2] Cyprian, *On Jealousy and Envy*, The Ante-Nicene Fathers, Vol 5, AGES, Edited By A. Roberts And J Donaldson, p. 1010

Christianity. And I was not only seeing the significance of His Command but also the consequences of its loss.

The adventure would only deepen in the months ahead.

CHAPTER 5

YOU CAN ASK A QUESTION

Since that morning when I made the declaration, "I'm ready to study the Bible," I had been able to think of little else than this profound personal discovery. Jesus' Command was becoming a significant part of my daily Christian journey. My yearlong season of recovery was now over. I was back with the congregation I had served for thirty-three years, only now I was working behind the scene to help position them for a future without me.

On a morning in February 2003, I awakened with a special sense of God's nearness. It was as if He had been whispering to me as I slept and awakened me with the words, *"You can ask a question!"*

On a conscious level, I wasn't even aware that I had a question to ask when I had gone to sleep the night before. Yet when I awakened and heard *"You can ask a question,"* I was immediately aware that I did have a question. It was a question that had been quietly demanding a hearing for months. In fact, it was a deep and troubling question, one that I had not had the courage to let fully surface in my mind, let alone ask God.

The reason for my struggle with this question was at least two fold. First, my discovery of Jesus' Commandment was having a profound impact on me. By this time, I had become fully persuaded that after believing in Jesus, guarding the Command He gave us was at the heart of true Christian discipleship. At the same time, some doubt had begun to gnaw away at the joy of this newfound understanding. And from this came the question.

> *How could Jesus give us only one command—to love one another as He had loved us—and not include loving God first?*

The second part of the question centered on what I had believed and taught for many years as Jesus' Command: "Love the Lord your God with all your heart and with all your soul and with all your mind . . . [and] love your neighbor as yourself."[1]

In my mind, I had been saying this: "If only Jesus had said, 'These are my *two* commandments. Love the Lord your God with all your heart and with all your soul and with all your mind, and love one another as I have loved you.' That would be so much easier for me to accept!"

I had even wondered if Jesus had in some way comprom . . . I couldn't even say it in my mind, for to say it would be to acknowledge that I doubted my Lord Jesus! Yet, I had clearly seen His Command, stated five times in His final message to the disciples.

> "A new command I give you: *Love one another.* As I have loved you, so you must *love one another.* By this all men will know that you are my disciples, if you *love one another.*"[2]

> "My command is this: *Love each other* as I have loved you."[3]

> "This is my command: *Love each other.*"[4]

---

[1] Matthew 22:37b, 39b
[2] John 13:34-35
[3] John 15:12
[4] John 15:17

I was torn between the New Command I was now seeing and the two commands I had always believed best summarized the Christian faith. Every time "the question" would attempt to surface, I would stuff it back into the corner of my mind, hoping that such an irreverent thought would not come to the attention of my Lord.

However, on this morning, I was awakened with a sense of His nearness and these words were clearly whispered to me. *"You can ask a question!"* In the moments in which all of this transpired, I didn't even have time to ask the question. Beyond that, I didn't *need* to ask it. To me, the invitation to ask the question revealed that the invitor *knew* the question already! Any response on my part was simply to acknowledge what He already knew. Now I simply let the question surface without attempting to cover it: *How could Jesus' Command be to love each other and not include loving God first?*

God's New Home

As I lay quietly on my bed in the minutes that followed, a stream of thoughts and Scriptures came flooding into my mind. First, I became aware that when Jesus gave us the New Commandment, He knew something we didn't know. (That may be the largest understatement in this book!) He *fully knew* the nature of the New Covenant that He had just introduced and would enact only hours later when He was crucified. His body would be broken and His blood shed. He would die on the cross and be buried. On the third day, He would be raised from the dead. Moreover, He *fully understood* that in this New Covenant, God would, for the first time in human history, *come to live in those who believed in Him.* Without a doubt, God had been *with* His covenant people in the past—in the cloud and pillar of fire, the Ark of the Covenant, and the magnificent Temple. He had also come *upon* them. But now He would make His home *in* His people.

I remembered that even as He introduced the New Commandment, Jesus spoke these words to His disciples: "And I will ask the Father, and he will give you another Counselor to be with you forever - the Spirit of truth." "you know him, for he lives *with* you and *will be in you.*"[1]

He continued by saying, "If anyone loves me, he will obey my teaching. My Father will love him, and *we will come to him* and *make our home with him.*"[2]

This astonishing reality was underlined in New Testament Scripture. In his first letter to the Corinthian believers, Paul the apostle said, "Don't you know that you yourselves are *God's temple* and that *God's Spirit lives in you?*"[3]

In his second letter, he continues, "for *ye are a sanctuary of the living God,* according as God said – "I will dwell *in*[4] them, and will walk among {them}, and I will be their God, and they shall be My people."[5]

Paul saw this as a very important part of the message God had sent him to deliver. He was bringing the answer to a "mystery that has been kept hidden for ages and generations, but is now disclosed to the saints . . . which is Christ *in you*, the hope of glory."[6]

---

[1] John 14:16, 17a, c
[2] John 14:23
[3] 1 Corinthians 3:16
[4] enoikeo - to inhabit Strong's New Exhaustive Concordance with Expanded Greek-Hebrew Dictionary
[5] 2 Corinthians 6:16 Young's Literal Translation, 1898
[6] Colossians 1:26, 27b

I was being reminded that because God would now live *in* those people that believed in Jesus, we would need to love Him in His place of dwelling—*in* those people who believed in Him. He was making Himself accessible to us *in* our brothers and sisters, but it would be impossible to love Him *in* them if we did not *love the brothers and sisters that He now lived in!* It was only when we "hugged" them that God would feel the squeeze!

Must Also Love His Brother

The second thing that came to my mind was the following words of Scripture:

> If anyone says, "I love God," yet hates his brother, he is a liar. For anyone who does not love his brother, whom he has seen, *cannot love God*, whom he has not seen. And he has given us this command: Whoever loves God *must also love his brother*.[1]

In that moment, it seemed clear to me that God was deliberately positioning Himself so we could *only* love Him by first loving our brothers and sisters that He now *lived in*. If I didn't love my brothers and sisters, it was impossible to "get to God" in order to love Him. The words *"cannot love* God" seemed extremely significant to me in that moment. More important than my screaming toward the stars in the night sky, *"I LOVE YOU, GOD!",* He was asking me to love my brothers and my sisters that were standing right next to me on planet earth and, in so doing, *love Him too as He now made His home in them.*[2]

---

[1] 1 John 4:20-21

[2] Just because God has chosen to live in the people who trust in Jesus Christ, that does not make them "God" nor does it make God "them."

You Visited Me

Then a third account from Scripture flooded my mind. It was from a question and answer session that Jesus was having with His disciples on the Mount of Olives. The dialogue had started when the disciples had called His attention to the massively impressive structure of the temple in Jerusalem. Jesus had responded by telling them that the building they were in awe of would soon be destroyed. That led them to ask a three-part question: "Tell us," they said, "when will this happen, and what will be the sign of your coming and of the end of the age?"[1]

As His answers unfolded, He told of a future time when He would return as King and peoples' ultimate destinies would be revealed.

> When the Son of Man comes in his glory . . . he will sit on his throne . . . and he will separate the people one from another as a shepherd separates the sheep from the goats. He will put the sheep on his right and the goats on his left.

> Then the King will say to those on his right, 'Come, you who are blessed by my Father; take your inheritance, the kingdom prepared for you since the creation of the world. For I was hungry and you gave me something to eat, I was thirsty and you gave me something to drink, I was a stranger and you invited me in, I needed clothes and you clothed me, I was sick and you looked after me, I was in prison and you came to visit me.'

> Then the righteous will answer him, 'Lord, *when* did we see you hungry and feed you, or thirsty and give you something to drink? *When* did we see you as a

---

[1] Matthew 24:3b

stranger and invite you in, or needing clothing and clothe you? *When* did we see you sick or in prison and go to visit you?'

The King will reply, 'I tell you the truth, *whatever you did for one of the least of these brothers of mine*, you did for me.'[1]

Suddenly, I was struck by the strength of His identification with His brothers and sisters, His New Covenant family—even the least of them. His identity as *being in them* was stronger than I had ever imagined. A closer look at what Jesus is saying reveals that I wasn't alone in my surprise.

The response of the righteous will be something like this; "Lord, I don't remember even *seeing* you, let alone *seeing you hungry, thirsty, lonely, needy, sick, or imprisoned!* How could I possibly have fed, clothed, or visited you?"

It's as if Jesus was saying, "Don't you remember that I had promised to *make my home in those who trust in me? Every act of love that you did to your brothers and sisters, you were actually doing to me. I was living right there inside of them.*"

This truth was affirmed in the New Testament letter to the Hebrews: "For God is not unfair. He will not forget how hard you have worked for him and how you have shown your love to him by caring for other Christians, as you still do. Our great desire is that you will keep right on loving others as long as life lasts . . . Then you will not become spiritually dull and indifferent."[2]

---

[1] Excerpts from Mathew 25:31-40
[2] Hebrews 6:10, 11a, 12a New Living Translation

One final image came flooding into my mind in those moments. It was a picture of me six months earlier standing at our kitchen range scrambling eggs. That's a story all of its own.

CHAPTER 6

A BREAKFAST SURPRISE

About four years after Patti and I were married, she was diagnosed as having a condition known as *hypoglycemia*, commonly known as "low blood sugar." To me, it was helpful information. It did explain why she would experience periodic waves of weakness. All her energy would seem to disappear, only to reappear a few hours later.

Her episodes of low blood sugar were less frequent in the years that followed and my awareness of her dietary needs faded into the background. At least, it stayed in the background for about a dozen years until our two children were old enough to have fully taken over their own breakfast duties. It was then that I became vaguely aware of a problem that Patti was experiencing.

I say *vaguely aware*, because by that time I was fully engaged as the senior pastor of a congregation. Actually, I need to be more explicit. I was pastoring a *growing church*. Those words had a special significance to me. I had been willing to pay the price in early morning prayer, endless breakfast and lunch appointments and meetings with key leaders and committees. In addition to weddings and funerals, there were my weekend responsibilities of overseeing three Sunday services, giving the sermon that was to inspire and nourish all those who were members of my congregation. (I will spare you the building programs, meetings with architects, city officials, planning commissions and government agencies.) It was very hard and yet very fulfilling work. Being a *successful* pastor was keeping me busy, occupied, challenged, and excited!

It was during this busy season of successful ministry that my wife started to call me from time to time late in the morning.

"I am so weak. Can you bring me something to eat?"

"Honey, what would you like? What can I bring you?"

"I don't know. I . . . I can't think. Anything!"

I loved my wife. I tried to be understanding. However, I was a very busy person. I didn't know if she fully understood how difficult it was for me to juggle appointments so I could respond to these interup-- . . . uh . . . calls for help. Being a good pastor, a good husband, a good father, a good neighbor, a good citizen, *a good everything*, was very important to me.

As Patti was eating the hamburger I had brought her, I would start the lecture.

"What did you have for breakfast?"

"I wasn't hungry when I got up. I didn't eat any breakfast."

"You really should know that you *have to* eat some breakfast or your blood sugar will drop!"

"I know, but I didn't have any appetite when I got up!"

This was repeated with increasing frequency over a period of months until a thought came to my mind. I controlled my own schedule. I got up very early, was out of the house, and at work before my wife was awake. What if I arranged my work schedule so I could come back to the house at about nine o'clock in the morning? I could cook breakfast for Patti, take some time to connect with her and then continue with the rest of my day.

It worked. My wife appreciated my coming home and having some time with her in the morning. She was glad to eat a couple of eggs with a slice of toast if I fixed it for her. Breakfast was easy for me. How long does it take to scramble a couple of eggs and toast a slice of bread?

Just this simple change turned out to be good for both of us. It gave me some time to connect with my wife early in the day. It helped Patti get her day started right. Most of the time, I did this new breakfast routine with a pretty good attitude. Now and then, I would feel pressured, inconvenienced, or taken advantage of by having to break into my day to make her breakfast. On those days, I could feel the tension in my face as I slid the plate of eggs and toast across the table.

"Can I get you anything else, Honey?"

"Could I have some jam for my toast?"

"Sure."

I was doing the right things. I was saying the right things; only on some days, I had to squeeze the words out between my teeth because my jaw seemed reluctant to open. But for the most part, it worked. In fact, Patti started to fix her own breakfast if I couldn't make it home or was out of town for a few days.

All that was years earlier. Now I was the one with the health issue, the needy one. After the first few months of my recovery had passed, I was surprised to discover that I enjoyed the simple task of cooking! Cooking seemed to awaken something creative inside me, something that was a part of finding myself again. With no fixed work schedule, making breakfast was easier than ever. I actually looked forward to it.

Now, the specific event that I was being reminded of on this special morning happened about eight months into my recovery. I was preparing breakfast for my wife one morning. Patti was sitting behind me at the kitchen table. I was standing at the kitchen range. I had just cracked a couple of eggs into a small mixing bowl and was preparing to blend them with a spoonful of cottage cheese. At that moment, I was surprised by a very clear whisper:

"Jesus came to your house for breakfast today."

It was that clear, that short, and that simple. The tone of the whisper was not abrupt or sharp. It was subdued, not drawing attention to the messenger but rather to the information that I needed to hear.

When I heard this whisper, I stood motionless, the fork that was in one hand resting in the unscrambled eggs in the bowl that was in my other hand. Tears began to fill my eyes. A clear message had been given to me. In the stillness of that moment, I was fully aware that there was only one person sitting at the table behind me waiting for breakfast. It was my wife. Yet in that same moment, I knew that I was about to scramble eggs for Jesus that morning.

Moments passed. As the tears began to clear from my eyes, I scrambled the eggs and then poured them into the waiting skillet. The toast popped up as I was turning the eggs for the final time. I slid them onto a plate and buttered the toast. I turned with the breakfast in my hand and took the half dozen steps from the kitchen range to our kitchen table. My wife looked up in anticipation of the steaming scrambled eggs and warm toast. I put the plate on the table in front of her.

"Here's breakfast, Babe. Can I get you anything else? Water?"

In that moment, it was clear to me that if I ever wanted to serve Jesus breakfast, I would never have a better opportunity than I did that morning.

It didn't happen overnight, but by the time a couple of months had passed, my attitude in serving my wife had changed. It wasn't just an emotion; it was the recognition that I had the opportunity to serve Jesus breakfast quite frequently. I even took out the garbage for Him a number of times when it was overflowing after breakfast was over.

It was many months before I told Patti what had happened to me that morning. In fact, it was not until I felt I was to share it publicly that I told her about making Jesus breakfast that day. Now she says it's one of the best messages she's ever heard me preach and she loves to hear me share it. Come to think of it, a lot of women seem to like that message.

I was beginning to see how strong the truth of God living in the people of faith really was! When I treated them with love, I was treating Him with love. And when I treated them carelessly and with indifference, I was treating Him carelessly and with indifference. This was becoming a clear reality to me as I was seeing the significance of Jesus' Commandment, "to love one another as He had loved us."

The sobering prophetic words that Jesus had given His disciples were impacting me with a weight I had never experienced before.

> 'I tell you the truth, whatever you did for one of the least of these brothers of mine, you did for me' and 'whatever you did not do for one of the least of these, you did not do for me.'[1]

---

[1] Matthew 25:40, 45

Two amazing truths were becoming clear to me; (1) *unless I loved my brothers and sisters*, I could not love God, and (2) when I loved my brothers and sisters, *I could not help but love God too!*

In the 1990's, my wife asked me to read *The Five Love Languages*, a book written by Gary Chapman.[1] It is a very insightful description of five ways we receive love from others: *words of affirmation, quality time, gifts, acts of service and physical touch*. He says that for each of us, one of these is our *primary love language*, the way we most naturally receive love.

My wife discovered that her primary love language is *quality time*. My primary love language is *words of affirmation*. As Chapman pointed out, sometimes we miss effectively communicating our love to another because we don't "speak" in the language our loved one understands best.

He was right. Many times, I had missed communicating my love to my wife in the language she understood best—*quality time*.

In the New Covenant, loving God is as important as it ever was. But how does He best receive our expressions of love? Is it sacrifices and offerings that God wants? Is He waiting to hear words of adoration from us? If so, I could spend hours shouting into the night sky "I love you, God! You are awesome!"

I think that means something to God, kind of like when your five year old child draws a picture of a heart on construction paper and then asks you to tell him the letters of the alphabet that spell "i LOve yUO." It's really special! However, there comes a point in parenting when we say to our precious little (or

---

[1] Gary D. Chapman, *The Five Love Languages,* 1992

big) children, "If you love Mommy (or Daddy), obey me when I tell you not to hit your sister. Treat her nice!"

I think that's what God was saying when He commanded us to believe in His Son, Jesus Christ, and listen to Him. When we believe in Jesus and listen to Him, we hear His Command to us. "My command is this: Love each other as I have loved you."[1]

To me, it seems that way God best receives love from us is through our *obedience* to Him. When we obey His Command to love another, we give God a double hug—the hug of obedience and then the hug He feels when we love those He now makes His home in. We should never forget that because God now lives in those who believe in Jesus, He can't help but "feel the squeeze" when we love one other.

So rather than shouting "I love you, God!" into the sky for hours, maybe I should give just a couple of shouts and then go back into the kitchen and help my wife clean up the pots and pans after dinner. Then I could give her some quality time. I would be speaking God's "love language"[2] and communicating my deep love for Him through my simple obedience to His command. Of course, my wife seems to like it too!

My question "How could Jesus give us only one command?" had been answered. In the New Covenant, loving God and loving your neighbor now centered on faith in Jesus Christ and the obedience that comes from faith—loving one another as He loved us.

In the back of my mind, I vaguely remembered reading something about the entire law being summed up in a single command. I'd need to look into that later, but for now, I was

---

[1] John 15:12
[2] Gary D. Chapman, *The Five Love Languages*, 1992

seeing Jesus' Command more clearly than I had ever seen it before.

> My command is this: Love each other as I have loved you.[1]

---

[1] John 15:12

CHAPTER 7

COMPARING THE OLD AND NEW

With some frequency, I'm asked the question, "What do you do?" I explain that I work with pastors and emerging leaders, and that I'm writing a book. Many times, the next question is, "What are you writing about?" I tell them that I'm writing about the Command Jesus gave us. Often, there is a brief pause and then a follow-up question: "Which command?"

That's a great question. For many Christians, Jesus' Command is "Love God with all your heart, soul and mind and love your neighbor as yourself." When I survey Christian congregations, over half of them give this as their answer. I certainly understand their response.

Many times, Jesus taught using parables, stories designed to get a point across to His followers. Sometimes the lesson was hidden within the story so only those that asked a follow-up question would get the answer. But there was one thing Jesus made very clear—His Commandment. He announced it in the clearest terms and then repeated it two more times on the night He gave it.

A new command I give you: Love one another. As I have loved you, so you must love one another.[1]

My command is this: Love each other as I have loved you.[2]

---

[1] John 13:34
[2] John 15:12b

This is my command: Love each other.[1]

Astonishingly, only one in ten Christians gives that as their answer! Most of us, and I was one of them, have substituted the two core commandments of the Old Covenant in place of the two core commandments of the New Covenant. In so doing, we crowd out the Command Jesus gave us. How did this come to be?

To find the answer to that question, I needed to take a closer look at the Old and New Testaments and the covenants and commandments they contained. First, I turned my attention to the Old Testament. For many, it is best known for the Ten Commandments, the ones written by God in stone and handed to Moses on Mount Sinai. For Orthodox Jews, the Old Testament contains 613 commands in what they call the Torah.

Are some of these commandments more significant than others? Apparently, Jesus thought so. One day an expert in the Law of Moses "tested him with this question."[2]

Teacher, which is the greatest commandment in the Law?[3]

Jesus answered him.

'Love the Lord your God with all your heart and with all your soul and with all your mind.' This is the first and greatest commandment. And the second is like it: 'Love your neighbor as yourself.' All the Law and the Prophets hang on these two commandments.[4]

---

[1] John 15:17
[2] Matthew 22:35b
[3] Matthew 22:36
[4] Matthew 22:37b-40

In giving him this answer, Jesus gave us the two core commandments of the Old Testament. These provide us with a very significant insight into the covenant that existed at that time, a covenant that would soon be made old by the introduction of the long promised New Covenant.

All that Jesus was, said, and did, converged when He introduced the New Covenant and gave us the New Commandment. The "new" was enacted in the hours that followed through Jesus' crucifixion, death, resurrection and a fresh infusion of the Holy Spirit. These realities are foundational to the Christian faith.

We know that while "the law was given through Moses; *grace* and *truth* came through Jesus Christ."[1] In this New Covenant, we are "not under law, but under *grace*."[2] As those that now live in a New Covenant and under *grace*, it seems reasonable for us to ask Jesus a question similar to the one asked by the above-mentioned expert in the Law of Moses. It would sound something like this.

> Teacher, what is the greatest commandment for those living in grace and truth?

Actually, Jesus gave us the answer to that question in two parts. The first half was given when He answered a question asked by someone in a crowd. "What must we do to do the works God requires?"[3]

For most of the people in the crowd, the way to be righteous and to please God was through works, obeying all of the commandments contained in the Law of Moses. Jesus' answer was surprisingly different.

---

[1] John 1:17b
[2] Romans 6:14b
[3] John 6:28b

> The work of God is this: to believe in the one he has sent.[1]

This is the first core commandment of Christianity. Believing in Jesus is at the heart of the New Covenant. Putting our trust in Him is where the Christian faith starts. Again, this is underscored when He spoke the first core commandment of the New Covenant in these familiar words.

> For God so loved the world that he gave his one and only Son, that whoever believes in him shall not perish but have eternal life.[2]

Later, Jesus gave us the second core commandment of the New Covenant.

> A new command I give you: Love one another. As I have loved you, so you must love one another. By this all men will know that you are my disciples, if you love one another.[3]

These core commandments of the New Covenant are expressed most succinctly in the words of John the Apostle in his first letter.

> we have confidence before God . . . because we obey his commands and do what pleases him. And this is his command: [1] to believe in the name of his Son, Jesus Christ, and [2] to love one another as he commanded us.[4]

---

[1] John 6:29b
[2] John 3:16
[3] John 13: 34-35
[4] 1 John 3:21b, 22b, 23

God, as the Father, commanded us *to believe in His Son, Jesus Christ*. Jesus, as God's Son, commanded us *to love one another*. Together, these are the core commandments of the New Covenant and of the Christian faith.

Now I recognized that both the Old Testament and the New Testament had core commandments. I had never seen them placed side-by-side. For the first time, I put them next to each other so I could contemplate their significance.

Core Commandments of the Old Covenant	**Core Commandments of the New Covenant**
(1) "Love the LORD your God with all your heart and with all your soul and with all your strength." Deuteronomy 6:5	(1) "For God so loved the world that he gave his one and only Son, that whoever believes in him shall not perish but have eternal life." John 3:16
(2) "love your neighbor as yourself." Leviticus 19:18b	(2) "Love one another. As I have loved you, so you must love one another. John 13:34

Does it matter which of these core commands I identified as applying most directly to me? Both from Scripture and from personal experience, I think it does. The two core commandments of the Old Covenant are rooted in *my finite* ability to love God and my neighbor.

(1) Love the LORD your God with all *your* heart and with all *your* soul and with all *your* strength.[1]

---

[1] Deuteronomy 6:5

(2) love your neighbor *as yourself*[1]

In contrast, the two core commandments of the New Covenant are rooted in *God's infinite love* for me.

> (1) For God so *loved* the world that he gave his one and only Son, that whoever believes in him shall not perish but have eternal life.[2]
>
> (2) *As I have loved you*, so you must love one another.[3]

Jesus' words, "as I have loved you," are very important in understanding the second core commandment in the New Covenant. Jesus told us that it was the love He received from His Father that enabled Him to love us. "As the Father has loved me, so have I loved you. Now remain in my love."[4] As we remain in His love, we are empowered to love one another.

In his first letter, John the apostle makes this important point very clear when he writes, "This is love: not that we loved God, but that he loved us and sent his Son as an atoning sacrifice for our sins." "We love because he first loved us."[5]

I now see this as a very significant difference between the Old Covenant and New Covenant. The New Covenant is rooted in God's *infinite love* for me rather than in my *finite love* for Him and my neighbor.

For many years, I believed in Jesus Christ and the New Covenant He enacted. Yet, I made the core commandments of the Old Testament the core commandments of my Christian faith: "'Love the Lord your God with all your heart and with all

---

[1] Leviticus 19:18b
[2] John 3:16
[3] John 13:34b
[4] John 15:9
[5] 1 John 4:10, 19

your soul and with all your mind and with all your strength' [and] 'Love your neighbor as yourself.'"[1]

At the same time, I struggled with a nagging sense that I wasn't really living up to what God expected from me. My responsibilities as a husband, father, son, friend, and pastor kept me from being as devoted to God as I wanted me to be.

Since my personal discovery of the core commandments of the New Covenant, that nagging sense is gone. In the process, I've gained some insight into why I struggled with my own spirituality for so many years.

In order to understand my struggle, think about this question with me. "If I love God with ALL of my heart, ALL of my soul, ALL of my mind and ALL of my strength, does that leave ANY of my heart, soul, mind, or strength with which to love others?"

For years, I subconsciously answered that question: "No, not if I'm doing it right!" I answered "No" because SOME of my heart, soul, mind and strength was being diverted to other things—my wife, my children, and people around me. "I should be spending *more time* in prayer and in the study of Scripture, doing the things that *really show* my love for God!"

From there, it was easy to internalize the following assumption: Whatever part of my love I reserve for others and myself was the measure of my personal failure to love God fully as I should. I disappointed (if not displeased) God when I saved some of that love for myself or others.

Then I saw the New Command that Jesus gave us.

> A new command I give you: Love one another. As I have loved you, so you must love one another. By this

---

[1] Mark 12:30, 31b

all men will know that you are my disciples, if you love one another.[1]

As I shared with you earlier, it was confusing for me at first. I don't think I was alone in this struggle. The tension between "love God with ALL" and "love one another like I have loved you" can be like trying to drive your car by pressing the brake pedal and accelerator at the same time!

Once again, let's look at the question and answer exchange between the expert in the Law of Moses and Jesus.

> One of [the Pharisees], an expert in the law, tested him with this question: "Teacher, which is the greatest commandment in the Law?" Jesus replied: "'Love the Lord your God with all your heart and with all your soul and with all your mind.' This is the first and greatest commandment. And the second is like it: 'Love your neighbor as yourself.' All the Law and the Prophets hang on these two commandments."[2]

Here are a few thoughts that helped me put Jesus' answer to the question about "the greatest command in the Law" in perspective.

First, Jesus was giving these words in answer to a question about the *Law of Moses* and the covenant that existed at that time. The man asking the question was an expert[3] in the Law of Moses. "Teacher, which is the greatest commandment in the Law?"[4] Jesus let him know that His two-part answer summed up all the commandments found in the *Law and Prophets*.[5]

---

[1] John 13:34, 35
[2] Matthew 22:35-40
[3] See Matthew 22:35
[4] Matthew 22:36
[5] See Matthew 22:40

Second, Jesus' two-part answer was not original to Him nor was it being spoken for the first time. As recorded in Luke's Gospel account, this two-part answer had already been spoken by a man[1] who was talking with Jesus. While it is not likely that this answer was new to this expert in the Law, it was the correct answer and one that may have already been accepted by the Jewish sect known as the Pharisees.

Third, Jesus never said that the two-part answer He gave was His Commandment. If He had wanted us to embrace His two-part answer as *His Commandment*, it would have been easy for Him to take this opportunity to communicate that to His disciples.

Fourth, Jesus never repeated this two-part answer again in any of His teachings. He merely answered the Pharisee's question about the Law and then moved on to other teachings.

Fifth, Jesus' two-part answer about the Law is not found in any of the New Testament Scriptures that followed. From its absence, it seems apparent that Jesus' disciples did not take His answer about the Law of Moses as one that should be repeated often and integrated into their New Covenant teaching.

Does that make "loving God" and "loving your neighbor" insignificant? Absolutely not! Jesus came to fulfill the Law. In the New Covenant, loving God is as important as it ever was! So is loving your neighbor.

Love for God has always been expressed by obedience to His commandments. In the New Covenant, we are free to love God with ALL our heart, soul, mind, and strength by obeying the Father's Command to believe in His Son and by obeying His Son's Command to love one another. These core

---

[1] See Luke 10:27

commandments of the New Covenant—(1) faith in Jesus Christ and (2) love for one another—only heighten our expression of love for God and for our neighbor. They fulfill and exceed the requirements of the Law given to Moses. Our obedience to them provides a clear and practical expression of our love for God and for our neighbor.

As I'm writing, my wife and I have been staying in the home of friends in Malibu while they are away on a short family vacation. Every morning I've been getting up early to write. Today, after writing for hours, I set my laptop aside and picked up a copy of the *LA Times*. The lead story in the second section was about life in a monastery in the high desert in southern California. The article[1] quotes the leader of the monastery.

> "We are here to have a quiet life and unite with God; there is no other reason to be here," he said. "I came because I felt I was distracted. I could not concentrate on the verse in the Bible that says you are to love the Lord your God with all your heart, all your soul and all your mind."

The reporter continues by writing, "The monks . . . focus entirely on worship, not on themselves or their surroundings. They pray for hours each day, reciting vast portions of Scripture from memory and endlessly repenting of their sins."

While I can certainly identify with the monks personal struggle, his words illustrate the dilemma that confronts a follower of Jesus who embraces the core commandments of the Law of Moses rather than the core commandments of the New

---

[1] David Kelly, *Los Angeles Times*, Monday, July 3, 2006, pp. B1, 10

Covenant. His attempt to love God with ALL his heart moved him toward isolation rather than into loving relationship with the larger family of believers.

From what I see in Christian history, this has been a common dilemma as early as the third century. While not the focus of this book, I have uncovered some interesting clues from church history as to how this happened. In short, this change corresponded to the loss of Jesus' Commandment in the teachings of the early fathers.

It is very difficult to make the core commandments from the Law of Moses the governing rule for Christian faith without displacing the core commandments of the New Covenant. It creates a tension that can actually move us away from the intended practice of loving one another. The antidote is for us to fully embrace the core commandments of the New Covenant—faith in Jesus Christ and love for one another.

For that to happen, we need to "make room on the table" for them. We have to recognize that the New Covenant and the Law of Christ fulfill the Old Covenant and the Law of Moses. Nothing is lost. Rather, what God has always desired is now fully realized in Jesus Christ and in those that trust in Him and obey His Commandment.

Personally, I now find that loving God and loving people flow much more seamlessly through my quiet times and busy times— my time alone and my time with others. Prayer and thanksgiving are less measured by the minute. Rather, the dialogue of prayer and praise starts when I awaken to the new day and end at sleep. My expressions of love for God are woven through "God and me" time and into "God and us" time with my brothers and sisters. Prayer and praise range from silent whispers of the heart to loud cries of desperation or gratitude, from spontaneous prayers to carefully written prayers to prayers that only the

Spirit knows. It's the closest I've come to prayer "without ceasing."[1]

If you have personally trusted in Jesus as your Savior and Lord, God now makes His home in you and in those around you who share this life of faith in Him. I encourage you to reverently release the former Covenant. Take your foot off the brake pedal! Fully embrace the New Covenant, the one enacted by your Lord and Savior, Jesus Christ. Trust Him completely! Love one another deeply! In so doing, you are obeying the Father's Command that we believe in His Son and His Son's Command that we love one another.

Remember, because God now lives in His New Covenant people, when we love one another, we love God too. This astonishing mystery was hidden in past ages but is now revealed. For this reason, Paul says that God had commissioned him to share "the word of God in its fullness -- the mystery that has been kept hidden for ages and generations . . . which is Christ in you, the hope of glory."[2] He now makes His home in those people who have put their trust in His Son, Jesus Christ!

Trust in Jesus Christ completely! Love one another deeply! This is the heart of Christian discipleship.

---

[1] 1 Thessalonians 5:17
[2] Colossians 1:25b, 26a, 27b

CHAPTER 8

THE TIME IS COMING

If I was going to understand the significance of the New Covenant, it would be helpful for me to have a clearer perspective on why there was even a need for this change. Wasn't the existing covenant good enough? Apparently not. Through His prophet Jeremiah, God promised a new covenant and it was the coming of the "new" that made the existing covenant "old" or "obsolete"[1] as the writer of Hebrews puts it.

The story of the Old Covenant is found in a body of writing known to Hebrew people as the Torah or Law. Christians know these same writings as the first five books[2] of the Old Testament and, along with the rest of the Bible, believe them to be sacred Scripture, inspired by God.

The Old Testament introduces God as the Creator. It tells of God's desire for relationship with the people He created. It also records special promises God made to Abraham, a man known for his amazing journey from Ur of the Chaldees (Iraq today) to a land that God said "I will show you" (modern day Israel). In it, God promises that Abraham would become known as the father of many nations. It also introduces us to Abraham's two sons, Ishmael and Jacob. It tells why God changed Jacob's name to Israel and of the dozen sons he fathered. The Torah also contains the story of Moses, famous for having been raised as an adopted son in Pharaoh's household and for leading his blood relatives, the children of Israel, out of Egypt after their four hundred year visit there had soured. However, Moses is most

---

[1] Hebrews 8:13
[2] The first five books of Old Testament are also known as the Pentateuch.

famous for having mediated a covenant between God and the Israelites and for bringing the Ten Commandments down from Mount Sinai.

The Old Testament records God's promise of a Messiah, the anointed One who would come to deliver the Israelites from their oppressors. It also tells how the Israelites, through disobedience to God's Commandments, broke the covenant He made with them. It records God's promise to give them a new covenant to replace the one they had broken.

The story of God giving the first covenant to Moses was of particular interest to me because of my desire to better understand the differences between the "old" and the "new." When Moses led Israel's descendants out of Egypt, their journey became known as the Exodus. Their amazing saga took them through the Red Sea and into the Sinai, an inhospitable wilderness that became their temporary home for forty years. It was there on Mount Sinai that God made a covenant with the children of Israel. He then gave Moses the Ten Commandments and all the rules that would govern their relationship with Him, one another, and the finer points of daily living. Here are the words of Scripture that tell of this significant event.

> In the third month after the Israelites left Egypt . . . they entered the Desert of Sinai, and Israel camped there in the desert in front of the mountain. Then Moses went up to God, and the LORD called to him from the mountain and said, 'Now if you *obey me fully and keep my covenant*, then out of all nations you will be my treasured possession. Although the whole earth is mine, you will be for me a kingdom of priests and a holy nation'.[1]

---

[1] See Exodus 19:1

After hearing these words, Moses came down from the mountain and brought this good news to the people.

> The people all responded together, 'We will do everything the LORD has said.' So Moses brought their answer back to the LORD.[1]

The Scriptures go on to describe what was happening on the mountain as this interchange between God and Moses was unfolding.

> Mount Sinai was covered with smoke, because the LORD descended on it in fire. The smoke billowed up from it like smoke from a furnace, the whole mountain trembled violently, and the sound of the trumpet grew louder and louder.[2]

God sent Moses back down to the people with instructions to warn them not to approach the mountain under penalty of death. Even an animal that strayed into the forbidden zone was to be killed.

The Israelite people were waiting at the foot of the mountain for Moses to return. The Scripture records their state of mind.

> When the people saw the thunder and lightning and heard the trumpet and saw the mountain in smoke, they trembled with fear. They stayed at a distance and said to Moses, "Speak to us yourself and we will listen. But do not have God speak to us or we will die."[3]

Moses tried to reassure them with these words.

---

[1] Exodus 19:8
[2] Exodus 19:18, 19a
[3] Exodus 20:18-19

> Do not be afraid. God has come to test you, so that the
> fear of God will be with you to keep you from sinning.[1]

You've probably heard the saying, "People run best scared."
While that might be true in the short run, it is seldom true over
the long run. Marathons are won by people that love to run, win
races, improve on their best time, hear the cheers of the fans,
and hold trophies in their hands. It's hard to scare someone
enough to win a marathon.

So it was with the Hebrew people. God gave the Ten
Commandments to Moses. He brought them down from the
mountain and taught them to the people. Their love for God was
to be expressed through obedience to His commands.
Disobedience to those commands was sin and was considered
hatred toward God.

They lived in a very black and white world. There was a
significant list of sins that had the death penalty written after
them, sins that quite a few of us have already committed. Sins
that were premeditated, done in anger or arrogance were treated
by God with special severity.

All of the people had given their word to Moses; "We will do
everything the LORD has said." But that was as they stood at
the base of a trembling mountain covered in smoke. Now they
were faced with actually keeping the Law with its Ten
Commandments. It was harder than they had ever imagined.
Some of their "best and brightest" failed miserably.

Take King David for example. David, the shepherd boy who
became King of Israel, was one of those whose failure was
particularly notable. While he is best known for his Psalms, the
Scriptures make no secret of the fact that David committed one
of the most shocking crimes of all the kings of Israel. He

---

[1] Exodus 20:20b

murdered a man in an attempt to cover an affair he had with the man's wife. The plot to murder the husband became necessary when the woman discovered she was pregnant because of their adulterous affair.

It would appear that the whole thing started innocently enough one spring evening when David couldn't sleep and went out on the rooftop patio of his palace to get some fresh air. It just so happened that his attention was drawn to a woman that lived in the neighborhood and was taking her post-menstrual purification bath as required by the Law. She was strikingly beautiful.

David sent one of his underlings to find out who she was. It turns out that she was the wife of one of his military men, Uriah. He was away fighting a war for King David.

As the old saying goes, "One thing led to another." Before it was over David had coveted his neighbor's wife, stolen her affection from her husband, and committed adultery with her. When she told David that she was pregnant by him, he lied to her husband—one of his most loyal and devoted soldiers— about his intentions in calling him back from the battlefield for some "rest and recreation." David's plan was that this brief interlude between Uriah and his wife would provide a logical explanation for the child that would be born months later.

However, out of loyalty to his fellow soldiers, Uriah would not sleep with his wife. When King David realized that his plan had failed, he sent Uriah back to the battlefront carrying his own death warrant. It contained sealed instructions from the King to the commander of the army ordering that Uriah be killed in battle. Yes, David murdered this loyal soldier in order to cover his own sin of adultery.

If I'm counting right, David broke five of the Ten Commandments. Two of the sins he committed had a mandatory death penalty.

> I. "If a man commits adultery with another man's wife -- with the wife of his neighbor -- both the adulterer and the adulteress must be put to death."[1]

> II. "If anyone takes the life of a human being, he must be put to death."[2]

The Scripture records the following account of what happened after David murdered the unsuspecting husband.

> After the time of mourning was over, David had her brought to his house, and she became his wife and bore him a son.[3]

Just in case you are wondering, David didn't end up getting the death penalty. As with most legal systems, there were safeguards and loopholes. "One witness is not enough to convict a man accused of any crime or offense he may have committed. A matter must be established by the testimony of two or three witnesses."[4] It seems that no one had actually *seen* David commit adultery or murder.

Be that as it may, no one would accuse King David of being insincere, a phony, a fraud, or a God-hater. Quite to the contrary, God describes David as "a man after his own heart."[5] The truth is that David failed miserably at keeping the Law.

---

[1] Leviticus 20:10
[2] Leviticus 24:17
[3] 1 Samuel 11:27a
[4] Deuteronomy 19:15
[5] 1 Samuel 13:14

Under the terms of the covenant, he deserved to die as a penalty for his sins.

The bottom line is this: the Law with its Ten Commandments and the fear of a death sentence wasn't enough to keep *even good people* from sinning. God's rules were being broken again and again.

Neither the people of that day nor those of us living presently should be surprised when God announced the coming of a new covenant. The reason for the new covenant, God said, was that the covenant He made with the children of Israel at Mount Sinai had been broken. It was broken by the people's failure to do what they had promised—to obey the commands it contained.

Something had to change. Through His prophets, God had begun to prepare the Israelites for the dramatic change that was coming. Here are the words God spoke through Isaiah, one of Israel's prophets, about 700 BC.

> Forget the former things; do not dwell on the past. See,
> I am doing a *new thing!*[1]

"Thing" is a word we use when we are being vague about that "something." I think this is what God was doing by using the word "thing." He wasn't ready to give them specifics but they did need to be prepared for the large change that was coming.

One hundred years after these words from Isaiah, God told them what this "new thing" would actually be. It was about 600 B.C. when God made this startling announcement through one of Israel's most well-known prophets, Jeremiah.

---

[1] Isaiah 43:18-19a

> "The time is coming," declares the LORD, "when I will make a *new covenant* with the house of Israel and with the house of Judah."[1]

The mysterious "new thing" Isaiah had foretold was no longer a mystery. A "new covenant" was coming! Every person of Hebrew descent should have sat bolt upright when they heard these words. Covenant was everything to them. Covenant defined how God related to them and how they were to relate to God. It was a binding legal agreement between God and His people.

The announcement came during a time of significant turmoil for the people to whom it was addressed. The fact is, they were a divided people, the "house of Israel"—ten of the twelve tribes living in the northern section of the land—and the "house of Judah"—the remaining two tribes living in the southern lands around Jerusalem. Furthermore, most of the Israelite people weren't even living in their beloved Promised Land. The armies of Assyria and Babylon had forcibly removed them. Only the poorest of them remained in Jerusalem and in the tribal territories that had been their home.

The announcement of a coming new covenant was the kind of news that should have been emblazoned in two-inch headlines on the front page of the *Jerusalem Daily* and the *Babylon Underground Review*—**GOD ANNOUNCES COMING NEW COVENANT!**

The fact that God would make a new covenant with them was extremely significant. A change in covenant would bring profound change for all of Israel, literally changing the rules by which they lived and worshipped God.

---

[1] Jeremiah 31:31

It was clear from the words "the time is coming" that this was something that would happen some time in their future. God was giving them advance notice. One thing was certain as they read the finer print. This covenant would be *different* from the existing one.

If I was going to understand the significance of the New Covenant, this is a point that I had to understand. This amazing difference is what we will consider next.

CHAPTER 9

NOT LIKE THE COVENANT

While I hadn't noticed this before, my attention was now gripped by a phrase spoken by Jeremiah, "not . . . like the covenant."[1] I had never really noticed how important this point was to God. When God wanted to announce the coming of a new covenant, this was the first thing He wanted Jeremiah to make clear to the people.

> "*It will not be like the covenant* I made with their forefathers when I took them by the hand to lead them out of Egypt, because they broke my covenant . . .," declares the LORD.[2]

The phrase "not be like" contains words of differentiation, words used to highlight the difference between the existing covenant and the one being announced. This was big—very big! There would be very significant changes in the new covenant that was now promised.

As I thought about this, I recognized that it wouldn't have made sense for God to do the same thing over again in light of the fact that the people had failed in their attempt to keep the existing covenant. Rather, they had broken the covenant. They had not done what they had promised to do when they stood at the foot of a trembling mountain years earlier; "We will do everything the LORD has said."[3]

---

[1] Jeremiah 31:32b
[2] Jeremiah 31:32
[3] Exodus 19:8b

Now they needed to be prepared for a significant change in the way they related to God and the way He related to them, a systemic change. In fact, Jeremiah had already given them one of the specific ways that the new covenant would differ from the existing one. It is found in the two sentences just before he announced the coming of a new covenant.

> In those days people will no longer say, 'The fathers have eaten sour grapes, and the children's teeth are set on edge.' Instead, everyone will die for his own sin; whoever eats sour grapes—his own teeth will be set on edge. The time is coming . . . when I will make a new covenant[1]

It seems that this saying, 'The fathers have eaten sour grapes, and the children's teeth are set on edge,' was quite popular among the people of Israel at that time. It was the way they expressed how the faux pas, moral deficiencies and maladaptive behaviors (the sins) of one generation penalized the next. The children's "deformed teeth" were a direct result of God's judgment for sins they had never committed—the sins of their fathers.

While that may seem unfair, there was good reason for them to attribute the deformed teeth of the children as the ill effects of the preceding generation's sin. It was part of the covenant God had made with them at Mt. Sinai. The second commandment went like this.

> You shall not make for yourself an idol . . . for I, the LORD your God, am a jealous God, *punishing the children for the sin of the fathers to the third and fourth generation*[2]

---

[1] Jeremiah 31:29-31a
[2] Exodus 20:4, 5

There it was in black and white—actually in stone. Under the existing covenant, the failure to love God by obeying His commands had dire consequences on the next three or four generations. The succeeding generations were punished for sins they had never committed. This was the rule mandated by God in the Ten Commandments given to Moses.

The thought of your children suffering as a consequence of your sin was one more deterrent to breaking God's Law. It made the fence between you and sinful behavior even more sharply barbed. Nevertheless, no promised punishment seemed large enough to prevent disobedience.

It is no wonder that David, in writing the Psalms, makes this appeal to God regarding the sins of previous generations.

> Do not hold against us the sins of the fathers; may your mercy come quickly to meet us, for we are in desperate need.[1]

Thankfully, the coming *new covenant* that Jeremiah was announcing would *not be like* the covenant God had made with their forefathers. This popular saying about "sour grapes" and "teeth set on edge" would no longer be relevant when this promised new covenant came. Jeremiah continues.

> Instead, everyone will die for his own sin; whoever eats sour grapes -- his own teeth will be set on edge.[2]

One of the prominent characteristics of the promised new covenant would be that each individual would bear the consequences of his own sin. The emphasis would be on personal responsibility and personal accountability.

---

[1] Psalm 79:8
[2] Jeremiah 31:30

This was only one of the ways that the new covenant would *not be like* the existing covenant. There was more fine print describing the features of the promised new covenant.

> I will put my law in their minds and write it on their hearts.[1]

God was saying that He would personally give His law to each participant in the new covenant. He would make it a part of their understanding by putting it in their minds and by writing it in the very core of their being—on their hearts.

This represented a dramatic change in the way God would communicate His laws to the people. Hundreds of years earlier when God had given His commandments to Moses on Mount Sinai, He had written the ten most important points in stone and given them to Moses to teach to the people. Here are the actual words that describe what happened.

> When the LORD finished speaking to Moses on Mount Sinai, he gave him the two tablets of the Testimony, the tablets of stone *inscribed by the finger of God.*[2]

In the promised new covenant, Jeremiah is saying that God would actually write His law on their hearts, not on stone tablets. What comes to my mind is that this new covenant would be characterized by a new level of connection—personal relationship—between the Creator God and each of the people that would live in this promised new covenant.

In the existing covenant, Moses had been the one person that had contact with God and then passed His words on to the rest of the people. The people actually wanted it this way. Moses was a go-between. However, that would change when the new

---

[1] Jeremiah 31:33b
[2] Exodus 31:18

covenant was enacted. Not only would there be a new level of personal accountability, there would be a new level of personal relationship between God and each of His people. Jeremiah's next words seem to confirm this.

I will be their God, and they will be my people.[1]

In this new covenant, there would be a sense of mutual ownership, God seeing them even more uniquely as *my* people and the people viewing their Creator as *my* God.

It got even better than that. Jeremiah continues to speak for God.

No longer will a man teach his neighbor, or a man his brother, saying, 'Know the LORD,' because they will all know me[2]

It is important to remember that this promise was being made to a communal people. This large ethnic nation was made up of the descendants of the twelve sons of Israel. They lived in family tribes. Unlike the communities that most of us live in today, their neighbors were their relatives, people that believed in the same God and lived under the same covenant. When God says, "no longer will it be necessary for someone to teach his neighbor or brother to know the LORD," He is not talking about a future world in which "everyone knows the Lord." Rather, He is talking about a covenant community where all the people of the community would know the Lord.

That "they will all know me" should not be considered a small improvement promised as part of the "new thing." Knowing God was not a common experience of those under the existing covenant. Even the priest and prophets struggled in their quest

---

[1] Jeremiah 31:33b
[2] Jeremiah 31:34c

to know God.[1] But this new covenant promised to take them to a new level of personal intimacy with God.

There was more. Jeremiah continues.

> they will *all* know me, *from the least of them to the greatest*," declares the LORD.[2]

All of His people in the new covenant would enjoy this promised personal intimacy with God. It would transcend age, gender, ethnicity, education, social status, and even spiritual office. God was saying that in the new covenant "they will *all* know me" and that included "*the least* of them to *the greatest*."

There was one final advantage to this promised new covenant.

> For I will forgive their wickedness and will remember their sins no more.[3]

Under the existing covenant given to Moses, there was a rigorous system of penalties and sacrifices for sin. The sacrifices usually consisted of some kind of animal being killed or symbolically banished, sent out alone into the wilderness to die. The penalties for sin—breaking one of the commands God had given them—ranged from ceremonial to severe and including a death sentence for a number of sins that are quite common to us today. The promise that God would "forgive their wickedness" and "remember their sins no more" was an incredible change and a huge benefit of the promised new covenant.

From even the small amount of information Jeremiah had given them, it seems that all would have eagerly anticipated the new covenant.

---

[1] 1 Samuel 3:7, Jeremiah 2:8, 4:22
[2] Jeremiah 31:34b
[3] Jeremiah 31:34c

God had spoken very clearly through Jeremiah. "The time is coming," declares the LORD, "when I will make a new covenant with the house of Israel and with the house of Judah."[1] No one knew how long it would actually be before the promised covenant would be enacted. The phrase *"new covenant"* was not recorded again in the Old Testament Scriptures. In fact, it would be six hundred years before the words *new covenant* would be heard again and recorded for us to see. They would be spoken on the eve of Passover in the year 33 A.D.

That's next.

---

[1] Jeremiah 31:31

CHAPTER 10

JESUS!

Six hundred years after Jeremiah announced the promise of a coming new covenant, Jesus was born in Bethlehem. His mother was Mary. Her husband was Joseph, a carpenter by trade. Jesus' earliest years were spent with Joseph and Mary in Egypt. When He was still a small child, they moved to Nazareth, a little village in the region of Galilee. No doubt, Joseph and Mary were regular worshipers at the small synagogue in Nazareth, making the young Jesus a familiar face to those who gathered there.

Even at an early age, Jesus showed an unusual aptitude in matters of the Jewish religion including an understanding of the Law and Prophets. That was demonstrated when Joseph and Mary took twelve-year-old Jesus with them on their annual pilgrimage to Jerusalem to celebrate the Passover.

When the Passover celebration had ended, the company of Jews who traveled together from the region of Galilee formed a caravan and started north toward home. Apparently, Joseph and Mary assumed that Jesus was with friends and family in the crowd of travelers. After a day of travel, they checked more closely and realized that he wasn't part of the crowd. It took them a day to get back to Jerusalem and a couple more days of searching the city before they found the missing boy. He was in the courts of the massive temple in Jerusalem, "sitting among the teachers, listening to them and asking questions. Everyone who heard him was amazed at his understanding and his answers."[1]

---

[1] Luke 2:46b-47

Mary was noticeably upset by the time they found him. Scripture records at least a part of the exchange that took place.

> When his parents saw him, they were astonished. His mother said to him, "Son, why have you treated us like this? Your father and I have been anxiously searching for you."[1]

Here is twelve-year-old Jesus' response to Joseph and Mary.

> Why did you seek Me? Did you not know that I must be about My Father's business?[2]

"My Father's business?" That should have been a clue that something unusual was happening with this boy. Apparently, Joseph and Mary didn't fully understand what he meant by that response. Be that as it may, he did return to Nazareth with them and seemed to be a model of obedience.

Nearly two decades later, there was an unusual stirring around the Jordan River. A Jewish prophet had come out of the desert with a fiery message of baptism for repentance and forgiveness of sins. Essentially, John the Baptist announced that he was getting people ready for what was coming next. What was coming next was more significant than anyone could have imagined. He used the words of one of Israel's prophets, Isaiah, to explain his mission.

> I am the voice of one calling in the desert, 'Make straight the way for the Lord.'[3]

---

[1] Luke 2:48
[2] Luke 2:49b NKJV
[3] John 1:23

Many people thought John was the long promised Messiah, the Christ. John firmly denied being the Christ but did say that there was someone coming soon, "the thongs of whose sandals I am not worthy to untie."[1]

Jesus was about thirty years old when he joined the crowds of people that were flocking to the edge of the Jordan to hear John the Baptist preach his fiery message and to be baptized by him.

> When all the people were being baptized, Jesus was baptized too. And as he was praying, heaven was opened and the Holy Spirit descended on him in the form of a dove. And a voice came from heaven: "You are my Son, whom I love; with you I am well pleased."[2]

It's worth noting that the first time we hear from Jesus, the twelve-year-old speaks of "my Father's business" and now come the words from the Father in heaven, "You are my Son. I love you. I'm pleased with you." Something new was in the air! Jesus is being presented to us as the "only begotten Son."[3]

Following the spectacular signs that accompanied Jesus' baptism, John the Baptist made a pivotal proclamation when he saw Jesus in the crowd the next day.

> Look, the Lamb of God, who takes away the sin of the world![4]

This was a startling statement, one that ties directly to the new covenant promised by Jeremiah six hundred years earlier. Through this prophet, the Lord had declared that He would "forgive their wickedness and . . . remember their sins no

---

[1] Luke 3:16b
[2] Luke 3:21-22
[3] John 3:16b New King James Version
[4] John 1:29b

more."[1] The implications of what John has just said are pivotal and reveal a central truth of the Christian faith.

John had more to say. He tells the crowd why he is so certain of the introduction he is making.

> Then John gave this testimony: "I saw the Spirit come down from heaven as a dove and remain on him. I would not have known him, except that the one who sent me to baptize with water told me, 'The man on whom you see the Spirit come down and remain is he who will baptize with the Holy Spirit.' I have seen and I testify that this is *the Son of God*."[2]

It was now official. Jesus was more than a boy in the temple with delusions of grandeur about his Father's business. God's voice was heard declaring that this was His Son whom He loved and with whom He was pleased. Now the respected prophet, John the Baptist, had added his testimony, "this is the Son of God." The people were being prepared for the *new thing* that had been promised by the prophets hundreds of years before.

John's introduction marked the beginning of Jesus' public notoriety. Jesus' teaching was accompanied by many miracles that demonstrated His power and attested to His credibility. His kindness and compassion as well as His willingness to speak truth were clearly demonstrated. During this time, His followers recognized him as the Messiah whose coming had been foretold by Israel's prophets centuries earlier. Even Moses had spoken of the coming of this one whose words none could afford to ignore.

> I will raise up for them a prophet like you from among their brothers; I will put my words in his mouth, and he will tell them everything I command him. If anyone

---

[1] Jeremiah 31:34b
[2] John 2:32b-34

does not listen to my words that the prophet speaks in my name, I myself will call him to account.[1]

Jesus' mission culminated three years later during the traditional Passover season. He and His closest followers, the handpicked twelve, were gathered in an upper room in Jerusalem to celebrate the historic Passover. This was the special meal that the Israelites had been instructed to eat on the night before they began their Exodus from Egypt over thirteen hundred years earlier. For the most part, they had celebrated the Passover annually and now Jesus and His disciples were celebrating it one more time.

On that night, six hundred years of silence regarding the promised new covenant would be broken. The New Covenant would be announced. But there would be more; a New Commandment would be given with it.

What happened in the hours that followed would change world history forever

---

[1] Deuteronomy 18:18, 19

CHAPTER 11

NEW COVENANT, NEW COMMANDMENT

For the first time, I was confronting the fact that Jesus announced the New Covenant and the New Commandment on the same night. Was this merely coincidental or did Jesus do this because He intended the New Covenant and the New Commandment to be linked?

I had never considered that possibility before. Now I had to know if Jesus intended for them to be connected. If He had, the importance of His Command was even more significant than I had thought. Beyond that, the loss of the Command was even more catastrophic than I had ever imagined. I needed to take a closer look at how they were introduced.

Possibly the most important truths that Jesus would ever give His disciples are found in the words He spoke to them on the eve of His crucifixion. Here is how I saw that pivotal night unfolding.

The Feast of Unleavened Bread had come and Jesus' disciples asked Him where they should plan to have the Passover meal. Here is Jesus answer:

> "Go into the city to a certain man and tell him, 'The Teacher says: My appointed time is near. I am going to celebrate the Passover with my disciples at your

house.'" So the disciples did as Jesus had directed them and prepared the Passover.[1]

When Passover evening arrived, "Jesus was reclining at the table with the Twelve."[2] As they were eating, Jesus "took bread, gave thanks and broke it, and gave it to them, saying, 'This is my body given for you; do this in remembrance of me.'"[3] Then He took the cup in His hand and made the proclamation.

> This cup is the *new covenant* in my blood, which is poured out for you.[4]

Jeremiah's promise, "the time is coming," had *now come!* The promised *New Covenant* would now be enacted. Six hundred years of Scriptural silence concerning the coming New Covenant was broken as Jesus spoke these words.

After they had eaten the meal, Jesus "showed them the full extent of his love."[5] He took off his street clothes, wrapped himself in a towel, and washed His disciples' feet. When Jesus had finished washing their feet, He told them that what He had just done for them was a model of servant-leadership they should follow.[6]

Next, He broke the startling news to them that one of them would turn on Him in an act of betrayal. It was only moments later that Judas hurriedly left the room, some thought in order to buy more food for the feast, and others assumed that he had gone to give urgently needed money to an impoverished citizen. After all, Judas was the treasurer for Jesus and the company of disciples.

---

[1] Matthew 26:18b, 19
[2] Matthew 26:20b
[3] Luke 22:19b
[4] Luke 22:20b
[5] John 13:1b
[6] See John 13:15-17

The events of this pivotal evening were now moving at a rapid pace. The vision of thirty pieces of silver was propelling Judas through the streets of Jerusalem toward those who had for months been seeking a way to arrest Jesus.

Jesus continued speaking to the eleven that remained. He explained that He would be leaving them and they could not go with Him on this journey. Having already announced the New Covenant in His blood, He now announces the New Commandment.

> A new command I give you: Love one another. As I have loved you, so you must love one another. By this all men will know that you are my disciples, if you love one another.[1]

Their obedience to this New Commandment, modeled after His love for them, would forever be the mark of authenticity by which people everywhere would identify them as His disciples—Christians in the modern vernacular.

Jesus repeats the New Command two more times before the night is over, only now owning it as *My Command*.

> My command is this: Love each other as I have loved you.[2]

> This is my command: Love each other.[3]

The promised *New Covenant* was now being enacted and the *New Commandment* had been given. In the past, this connection had never been clear to me. Now I saw the unmistakable link,

---

[1] John 13:34, 35
[2] John 15:12
[3] John 15:17

one that was central to authentic Christianity. *The New Covenant came with the New Commandment.* The connection between them seemed too obvious to miss.

Astonishingly, through decades of Christian ministry and teaching, the New Covenant and the New Commandment had never been connected in my own thinking and theology. Now it seemed undeniable to me. Jesus had intentionally linked the New Covenant and the New Commandment by introducing both of them on this pivotal night! The New Covenant and the New Commandment were as inseparable as the Ten Commandments were to the covenant God made with the Israelites at Mount Sinai.

As Christians, we readily embrace the following "new" elements.

New Covenant –

> he took the cup, saying, "This cup is the *new covenant* in my blood, which is poured out for you.[1]

New Birth –

> Praise be to the God and Father of our Lord Jesus Christ! In his great mercy he has given us *new birth* into a living hope through the resurrection of Jesus Christ from the dead[2]

New Creation –

> Therefore, if anyone is in Christ, he is a *new creation*; the old has gone, the new has come![3]

> Neither circumcision nor uncircumcision means anything; what counts is a *new creation.*[1]

---

[1] Luke 22:20b
[2] 1 Peter 1:3
[3] 2 Corinthian 5:17

New Life –

We were therefore buried with him through baptism into death in order that, just as Christ was raised from the dead through the glory of the Father, we too may live a *new life.*[2]

New Man –

His purpose was to create in himself *one new man* out of the two, thus making peace, and in this one body to reconcile both of them to God through the cross, by which he put to death their hostility.[3]

New Self –

put on the *new self,* created to be like God in true righteousness and holiness.[4]

New Way of the Spirit –

But now, by dying to what once bound us, we have been released from the law so that we serve in the *new way of the Spirit,* and not in the old way of the written code.[5]

As a part of my journey of discovery, I could no longer ignore the **New Command** He gave us. It was the one commandment He owned as "My Command" and the one that He identified as the mark of authenticity on those who would follow and learn of Him!

---

[1] Galatians 6:15
[2] Romans 6:4
[3] Ephesians 2:15b, 16
[4] Ephesians 4:24
[5] Romans 7:6

New Commandment –

> A *new command* I give you: Love one another. As I have loved you, so you must love one another. By this all men will know that you are my disciples, if you love one another.[1]

Many of us as Christians embrace the New Covenant but then awkwardly link it with the Commandments that were given with the Old Covenant. In so doing, we attempt to live in two covenants at once—something that is impossible to do. We live in what I've come to think of as a "no man's land" between the two covenants, vulnerable to confusion and condemnation. We miss the empowerment that comes through grace and the powerful simplicity of the "new."

The Ten Commandments given by Moses were written in stone and carried in the Ark of the Covenant—God's dwelling place in that day. The One Commandment given by Jesus is now written on the hearts of those who believe in Him and is carried there inside of them—God's dwelling place in this day. As Jeremiah had promised long ago, in this new covenant God has not only written the Law on our hearts but put it in our minds as well.

> "This is the covenant . . .," declares the LORD. "I will put my law in their minds and write it on their hearts. I will be their God, and they will be my people. No longer will a man teach his neighbor, or a man his brother . . ."

Isaiah, too, had foretold this when he wrote, "All your sons will be taught by the LORD, and great will be your children's peace."[2] Jesus had quoted these words in His teaching when He said, "It is written in the Prophets: 'They will all be taught by

---

[1] John 13:34, 35
[2] Isaiah 54:13

God.' Everyone who listens to the Father and learns from him comes to me."[1]

As I searched the Scriptures, I found only one other place that seemed to match these prophetic declarations. It was written seven hundred years after Isaiah had first said, "all your sons will be taught by the LORD . . ." I discovered it in Paul's first letter to the Christians in Thessalonica. He wrote, ". . . you yourselves have been taught by God . . ."[2]

What lesson was so important to God that He would *personally* teach it—put it in their mind—and *personally* inscribe it—write it on their hearts? Paul goes on to tell us what that lesson was.

> Now about brotherly love we do not need to write to you, for you yourselves have been *taught by God to love each other.*[3]

I was astonished to see what I had never comprehended before. Jesus' Command was the lesson God personally taught and inscribed on their hearts: "Love each other!" This is what the prophets had foretold. The promised New Covenant had been given and God was now teaching the New Commandment. This time, He was writing it "not with ink, but with the Spirit of the living God, not in the tablets of stone, but in fleshy tablets of the heart . . ."[4]

The covenant God made at Mount Sinai is linked with the Ten Commandments He gave through Moses. The New Covenant God made in Jerusalem is linked with the One Commandment Jesus gave on the eve of His crucifixion. The New Covenant

---

[1] John 6:45
[2] 1 Thessalonians 4:9b
[3] 1 Thessalonians 4:9
[4] 2 Corinthians 3:3b

and the New Command are inextricably linked. They are inseparable!

CHAPTER 12

ONE NEW PERSON

I could now see more clearly than ever the "new" that was emerging out of the "old." The New Covenant that God promised to Israel was to be fully embraced by the Hebrew people. It was *their New Covenant*. However, the New Covenant was not for them alone. Other nations, those known as Gentiles, were invited to share in the amazing provisions that were now given to God's New Covenant people. Jews and Gentiles would now be united as one family of faith, children of the Heavenly Father.

A "new person" was being created. A new unity was being forged. Through Jesus, God's "purpose was to create . . . *one new man* out of the two, thus making peace, and in this one body to reconcile both of them to [Himself] through the cross, by which he put to death their hostility."[1]

This inclusion of the Gentiles was part of the "new thing" that had been promised by the Prophets for hundreds of years. King David was one of those that foretold this "new thing" in his poetic and prophetic Psalms. He said that Israel's song of worship to God—the solo they had sung—would someday become a chorus, the voices of the nations! It would require that they sing *a new song*.

> Sing to the LORD a *new song*; sing to the LORD, *all the earth*. Sing to the LORD, praise his name; proclaim his salvation day after day. Declare his glory among the *nations*, his marvelous deeds among *all peoples*.

---

[1] Ephesians 2:15b, 16

> Ascribe to the LORD, O families of *nations*, ascribe to the LORD glory and strength. Say among the *nations*, "The LORD reigns."[1]

The word *nations—gowy* in Hebrew—referred to the Gentile ethnicities on the earth, the people that had previously worshiped idols they had made with their own hands. In the New Covenant, these nations would be invited to join those that had lived under the covenant given by God through Moses.

Jesus spoke of this enlarged company of covenant people to those Jews that followed Him.

> I am the good shepherd; I know my sheep and my sheep know me . . . and I lay down my life for the sheep. *I have other sheep* that are not of this sheep pen. I must bring them also. They too will listen to my voice, and *there shall be one flock and one shepherd.*[2]

The two—Jews and Gentiles—would become *one flock with one shepherd.* Paul, the apostle to the Gentiles, explains this amazing change and God's plan to join the two ethnicities into "one new man" in the New Covenant in these words.

> Therefore, remember that formerly you who are Gentiles by birth . . . were *separate* from Christ, *excluded* from citizenship in Israel and *foreigners* to the covenants of the promise, without hope and without God in the world. But now in Christ Jesus you who once were far away have been brought near through the blood of Christ. For he himself is our peace, who has made the two one and has destroyed the barrier, the dividing wall of hostility, by abolishing in his flesh the law with its commandments and regulations. His

---

[1] Psalm 96:1-3, 7, 10a
[2] John 10: 14, 15b, 16

purpose was to create in himself *one new man out of the two*, thus making peace, and in this one body to reconcile both of them to God through the cross, by which he put to death their hostility. He came and preached peace to you who were far away and peace to those who were near. For through him we both have access to the Father by one Spirit. Consequently, you are *no longer foreigners and aliens*, but fellow citizens with God's people and members of God's household, built on the foundation of the apostles and prophets, with Christ Jesus himself as the chief cornerstone. In him the whole building is joined together and rises to become a holy temple in the Lord. And in him you too are being built together to become a dwelling in which God lives by his Spirit.[1]

This was a very large change. Now all who believed the message and trusted in the Messiah would become members of a new household, God's household. Jews and Gentiles would be joined in one family as brothers and sisters—the children of one Father.

The New Commandment was an indispensable part of that plan. It was imperative that they "love one another as He had loved them" for the wonder of the New Covenant to be demonstrated! This was indeed God's plan and purpose for His people. The Jews, those who had formerly lived under the Law and Covenant given through Moses, would embrace the New Covenant and the New Commandment. For them, the writer of Hebrews describes the change in these words.

By calling this covenant "new," he has made the first one obsolete; and what is obsolete and aging will soon disappear.[2]

---

[1] Ephesians 2:11-22
[2] Hebrew 8:13

Those who had lived under the covenant given at Mount Sinai would now release it in order to embrace the New Covenant.

It would be a large change for the Gentiles also, those that had lived without God's Law. They could no longer be a lawless people. Those Gentiles that put their faith in Jesus Christ would now be called to embrace the Law of Christ—the New Commandment.

Together, Jews and Gentiles would live in the New Covenant. They would put their faith in Jesus the Messiah, "the Lamb of God, who takes away the sin of the world!"[1] Together, they would live in the Law of Christ and guard the One Commandment that it contained: "As I have loved you, so you must love one another."[2]

---

[1] John 1:29b
[2] John 15:12b

CHAPTER 13

LOST AND FOUND?

It was now clear to me that there was a strategic connection between the One Commandment Jesus gave us and all of the teaching about love in the rest of the New Testament. Jesus is the founder of Christianity. It only makes sense that we should look to Him as the source of the foundational truths of the faith that bears His name.

Discovering the connection between Jesus' Commandment and the instruction about love in the rest of the New Testament has been a very significant part of my journey of discovery. I now see that because these early disciples knew His Commandment, their teaching about love was not just another subset of doctrinal truth. Rather, their New Testament letters are like a thick forest of applications about how we are to *relate to one another in love*. They are brimming with insights concerning *what is* and *what is not* loving behavior.

Why didn't I make that connection earlier? I see a number of reasons for this. First, I simply did not *see* Jesus' Command as a *real commandment*. Rather, I viewed it as one more truth in a series of teachings that Jesus gave to His disciples. I now see that while all truth in the Bible is equally true, not all truth is equally important. When Jesus said, "This is my command," He was assigning it the highest priority among the things He taught us.

Second, I had not consciously made the connection between the New Covenant and the New Commandment. The fact that Jesus announced them both on the same night had not been clear in my mind or my theology. I did not see them as being inextricably linked.

Third, I did not understand the connection between covenant and commandment in Hebrew history. That connection was understood and assumed in Judaism, a connection so close that the Ten Commandments given by God to Moses were literally kept inside of the Ark of the Covenant. In fact, the Ten Commandments were the *words of the covenant.* That is clear from the Torah.

> Moses was there with the LORD forty days and forty nights . . . [and] he wrote on the tablets the *words of the covenant -- the Ten Commandments.*[1]

> There was nothing in the ark except the two stone tablets that Moses had placed in it at Horeb, where the LORD made a covenant with the Israelites after they came out of Egypt.[2]

Now I clearly saw that *covenant* and *commandment* were always connected. This was taking on new and strategic importance in my thinking.

Fourth, I did not see the Commandment Jesus gave us as the source, the fountainhead, out of which the vast amount of teaching about loving one another in the New Testament came. I now see that Jesus, as the "author and finisher of our faith,"[3] would naturally be expected to be the source and initiator of such a central truth in the Christian faith.

---

[1] Exodus 34:28a, c
[2] 1 Kings 8:9
[3] Hebrew 12:2b King James Version

I had come face to face with my personal loss of Jesus' Command. I had also been stunned by the loss of His Command by the early church fathers (125 – 325 A.D.).

That brought me to another important question: If the Command Jesus gave us was *lost* early in this journey, was it *rediscovered* at some point during the last eighteen hundred years of church history?

That question propelled me into long hours of searching church history. I discovered that I wasn't alone in my oversight of this pivotal command. Many of the powerful messages about love in our long Christian history also failed to make a direct connection between Jesus' Command and the many references to love in the balance of the New Testament Scriptures.

Augustine of Hippo is a very significant figure in Christian history, in my opinion the most influential in the last sixteen hundred years. Some have called him the father of theology. Having both a powerful testimony of conversion and a brilliant mind, he was a prolific writer. His insight into Jesus' Command is visible in his lecture on John 13:34-35 in the year 416 A.D.

> THE Lord Jesus declares that He is giving His disciples
> . . . a new commandment, that we should love one another, as He also hath loved us. This is the love that renews us, making us new men, heirs of the New Testament, singers of the new song. It was this love, brethren beloved, that renewed . . . the blessed apostles: it is . . . now renewing the nations, and from among the universal race of man . . . is making and gathering together a new people, the body of the newly-married spouse of the only-begotten Son of God . . . renewed
> . . . by the new commandment

In my mind, finding these words represented one of the most hopeful moments in my search. However, this was point one in his lecture that day. Then came point two.

> Think not then, my brethren, that when the Lord says, "A new commandment I give unto you, that ye love one another," there is any overlooking of that greater commandment, which requires us to love the Lord our God with all our heart, and with all our soul, and with all our mind; for along with this seeming oversight, the words "that ye love one another" appear also as if they had no reference to that second commandment, which says, "Thou shall love thy neighbor as thyself." For "on these two commandments," He says, "hang all the law and the prophets."[1]

Unfortunately, it was point two that would carry the day for Augustine. He repeated this two-part summary of the Law of Moses over twenty times in his writings. In his mind and theology, Jesus two-part answer to a question about the Law of Moses overshadowed the New Command Jesus gave us and owned as "My Commandment."

While Jesus said that all the Law and Prophets hung on the two commands—to love God and love for our neighbor—it appears that Augustine took the liberty to hang the New Testament on them as well.

> For this love embraces both the love of God and the love of our neighbor, and "on these two commandments hang all the law and the prophets," we may add the Gospel and the apostles.[2]

---

[1] St. Augustin: *Homilies On The Gospel Of John*, The Nicene And Post Nicene Fathers, Volume 7, *Philip Schaff, editor*, AGES, pp. 636-637

[2] St. Augustin: *The Enchiridion*, The Nicene And Post-Nicene Fathers, First Series, Volume 3, Philip Schaff, editor, AGES, p. 542

"We may add the Gospel and the apostles?" Personally, I found it troubling that Augustine would make this addition. Why would he put the Law and Prophets above the Gospel? The writer of Hebrews says that "In the past God spoke to our forefathers through the prophets at many times and in various ways, but in these last days he has spoken to us by his Son, whom he appointed heir of all things, and through whom he made the universe."[1] Yet it seemed to me that Augustine struggled to give the New Command, the one that Jesus owned as His Command, its rightful place in New Covenant theology. A hopeful moment of recovery for Jesus' Command was missed. One of the most eminent voices in our long Christian history had spoken with an uncertain sound, a sound that carried well throughout church history.

Next, I searched the *Canons and Dogmatic Decrees from the Seven Councils* of the church spanning the fourth through eighth centuries. I found no direct reference to Jesus' Command.

Then I looked to the Reformation period of the 1500's. There were hopeful moments when it looked as if Jesus' Command had been rediscovered and that recovery would soon follow. We are indebted to Martin Luther for translating the New Testament from Latin into the language of his day. He showed profound insights into Jesus' Command as he expounded the Scriptures that he had come to treasure.

Yet one of his most lasting legacies was the Augsburg Confession. Would it bring a rediscovery of the Command? I think not. While Luther had at times taught convincingly on Jesus' Commandment, the Augsburg Confession focused on the important *first core commandment* of Christian discipleship— faith in Jesus Christ. It contained over one hundred references to *faith, belief,* or *trust* in God but mentioned *love* only three times

---

[1] Hebrews 1:1, 2

and *charity* only three times, but none of them in direct reference to the Command Jesus gave us.

In general, Luther's Augsburg Confession (1530) became the doctrinal foundation for the Anglican Church, the Methodist Church, the holiness movement, and Pentecostal movement. To their credit, they inherited the emphasis on faith contained in the Augsburg Confession but also inherited the absence of the important *second core commandment*—Jesus' Command that we love one another as He had loved us.

Of all the branches of the Reformation, the Anabaptists[1] had the clearest grasp of Jesus' Commandment. Their teachings were more rooted in Jesus' words as recorded in the Gospels and less influenced by the writings of the early fathers and church theologians that followed.

They started well; however, for some in their ranks, "The Rule of Christ"[2] won out over the Command of Christ. The Rule of Christ was their title for the four-step plan based on Matthew 18:15-17, a plan that culminated in shunning those who violated the tenants of their faith. Over time, this resulted in many divisions among them over speculative doctrines and led to painful wounds among sincere believers.

To their credit, some of the branches of the Mennonites (Anabaptist) still make direct reference to Jesus' Command in their contemporary statement of faith and practice. (As difficult as I found it to believe, direct reference to Jesus' Command is not found in the statement of faith in the majority of western denominations existing today.)

---

[1] "a member of any of various Protestant sects, formed in Europe after 1520, that denied the validity of infant baptism, baptized believers only, and advocated social and economic reforms as well as the complete separation of church and state." (Random House Webster's Unabridged Dictionary)
[2] Robert Friedmann, *The Theology of Anabaptism*, p. 43

John Calvin's brilliant mind and outstanding education enabled him to make very profound and hopeful commentary on Jesus' Command. I found his writings on John's Gospel and first letter to be some of the most inspiring of all. Yet he seemed to lack a practical application of this precious truth in his personal life and in the church he oversaw in Geneva. In practice, he appeared to favor the Law of Moses over the Law of Christ.

One of Calvin's most influential works was *The Institutes of the Christian Religion,* a book he labored over for much of his adult life. First published in 1536, the final edition was released twenty-three years later in 1559. It has been a guiding light for many in the Reformed wing of Protestantism over the past 450 years. While it is nearly seventeen hundred pages in length, Calvin makes no direct reference to Jesus' Commandment within its pages, an omission that reinforces my earlier observation.

It is hard to find a major figure in church history that stressed the importance of Christian love more than John Wesley did. As I searched through eleven thousand pages of his sermons, journals, letters and commentaries, his passion is very clear. I think Wesley's favorite verse on loving one another was taken from John the apostle's first letter, "Beloved, if God so loved us, we ought also to love one another."[1]

The importance of loving one another was so woven through the fabric of Wesley's life that I found it even in the grammar lessons he wrote.

---

[1] 1 John 4:11 King James Version

> A Verb must always be of the same Number and Person with the Noun or Pronoun going before it; as, "I love you." "Christians love one another."[1]

Wesley's true passion is revealed in his commentary on John's words in his first letter, "this is his command: to believe in the name of his Son, Jesus Christ, and to love one another as he commanded us."[2] Wesley wrote the following.

> And this is his commandment — All his commandments in one word. That we should believe and love — in the manner and degree which he hath taught. This is the greatest and most important command that ever issued from the throne of glory. If this be neglected, no other can be kept: if this be observed, all others are easy.[3]

In spite of Wesley's passionate pleas for believers to love one another, he lamented the lack of love that he saw in many who professed Christian faith. He longed for a return to the days when observers would again say, "See how they love one another."

While I found five direct references to Jesus' Command in his writings, Wesley did not cite the Command as the primary text for any of his 141 sermons we have recorded. Wesley's brief commentary on John 13:34 seems understated, a probable indicator of why he never used it as the primary text in any of the sermons he left us.

---

[1] *The Works of John Wesley*, Third Edition , Volume XIV, Grammars, Musical Work, Letters, 1872 Edition, p. 18
[2] 1 John 3:23
[3] John Wesley, *Notes On The Whole Bible*, AGES, p. 832

I came to the sad conclusion that I was not alone in my oversight of Jesus' Command. By and large, love has been a *subset* of Christian truth and teaching. It has not been viewed as a *core commandment* of authentic Christianity. I believe we have failed in large part to grasp the co-centrality of the Command God the Father gave us—to believe in His Son, Jesus Christ—and the Command that Jesus the Son gave us—to love one another as He loved us. As stated earlier, we find this most clearly presented in the following words.

> And this is his [God's] command: to believe in the name of his Son, Jesus Christ, and to love one another as he [Jesus] commanded us.[1]

The night Jesus gave us the New Commandment, He repeated the phrase *love one another* five times in His final message to the disciples!

> "A new command I give you: *Love one another*. As I have loved you, so you must *love one another*. By this all men will know that you are my disciples, if you *love one another*." "My command is this: *Love each other* as I have loved you." "This is my command: *Love each other*."[2]

All of the teaching about *love for one another* that is found in the New Testament letters naturally and rightfully flows out of the One Command that Jesus gave us. While this is built on all that God had communicated in the Old Testament, Jesus called it a *new* commandment. It's important that we do not leave the impression that the Christian doctrine about love is primarily ours from the Old Testament *or* from Peter, James, John, or Paul. Jesus is the author of Christianity. He made love *His*

---

[1] 1 John 3:23
[2] See John 13:34, 35; 15:12, 17

Commandment! He also established Himself as the standard and model of what *loving one another* is to look like.

Here is a mosaic of the *"love one another's"* that flow out of Jesus' Commandment and are found in the New Testament letters.

"Be devoted to one another in *brotherly love*. Honor one another above yourselves." "Let no debt remain outstanding, except the continuing debt to *love one another . . .*" "he who *loves his fellowman [another]* has fulfilled the law." "do not use your freedom to indulge the sinful nature; rather, *serve one another in love.*" "Be completely humble and gentle; be patient, *bearing with one another in love.*"

"May the Lord make *your love increase* and overflow for each other . . . " "Now about *brotherly love* we do not need to write to you, for you yourselves have been taught by God to *love each other.*" "your faith is growing more and more, and *the love every one of you has for each other* is increasing." "And let us consider how we may spur *one another on toward love* and good deeds."

"Keep on *loving each other* as brothers." "Now that you have purified yourselves by obeying the truth so that you have *sincere love for your brothers, love one another* deeply, from the heart. For you have been born again . . ." "*Love the brotherhood* of believers . . ." "*love as brothers*, be compassionate . . ."

"Above all, *love each other* deeply, because love covers over a multitude of sins." "Greet one another with a *kiss of love.*" "make every effort to add to your faith . . . brotherly kindness; and to brotherly kindness, *love.*" "This is the message you heard from the beginning: We should *love one another.*" "And this is his command: to believe in the name of his Son, Jesus Christ, and to *love one another* as he commanded us."

"Dear friends, let us *love one another*, for love comes from God. Everyone who *loves* has been born of God and knows God." "Dear friends, since God so loved us, we also ought to *love one another.*" "No one has ever seen God; but if *we love one another*, God lives in us and his love is made complete in us." "I am not writing you a new command but one we have had from the beginning. I ask that we *love one another.*"[1]

With this as the backdrop, I needed to take a new look at the New Testament. I discovered that its familiar passages took on new meaning to me as a result of my personal discovery of the Command Jesus gave us.

---

[1] John 13:34a, 34b, 35, 15:12, 15:17, Romans 12:10, 13:8a, 8b, Galatians 5:13b, Ephesians 4:2, 1 Thessalonians 3:12, 4:9, 2 Thessalonians 1:3, Hebrews 10:24, 13:1, 1 Peter 1:22-23a; 2:17b; 3:8b; 4:8, 5:14a; 2 Peter 1:5b, 7b; 1 John 3:11, 23, 4:7, 11, 12, 2 John 1:5b

CHAPTER 14

THE KING'S LAW

I found myself thinking about the large transition that had been made by those first believers in Jesus as the Messiah. They were stepping out of the familiar, what they had known for centuries, to embrace the "New." Both the size and significance of this change cannot be overestimated.

In one of His first lessons, Jesus had pointed out how difficult this change was for the Hebrew people. He did it with a story about wine and the wineskins that contained it.

> And no one pours new wine into old wineskins. If he does, the new wine will burst the skins, the wine will run out and the wineskins will be ruined. No, new wine must be poured into new wineskins. And no one after drinking old wine wants the new, for he says, *'The old is better.'*[1]

Yet, those who believed the message that Jesus brought were being asked to choose the "new" over the familiar and well-aged "old." It was a new season. New wineskins would be filled with a fresh infusion of the Spirit. The Holy Spirit would empower the people of the New Covenant to live in the heavenly culture of a coming Kingdom. Moreover, with the promised New Covenant and New Command, the sacred Old Testament Scriptures would soon be joined by New Testament Scriptures.

Many believe that the first New Testament Scripture written was the letter James sent to "the twelve tribes scattered among the

---

[1] Luke 5:37-39

nations."[1] Even if it wasn't the first, it is agreed that it was written early—possibly predating all of the Gospel accounts. What is certain is that it was written *before* John's gospel and his letters, those that give us the clearest statement of the Command Jesus gave.

James had emerged as the overseer of the church in Jerusalem, the earliest and most Jewish Christian congregation. The members of the Jerusalem congregation had known only the Law of Moses before believing in Jesus as Messiah. James was confronted with the challenge of pastoring the first believers that would be governed by the long promised, but freshly enacted, New Covenant.

In my thinking, James was at a bit of a disadvantage for the role he had been given. He was known as *James the younger.*[2] He was not one of the twelve Jesus had tutored for three years. (Jesus had chosen two others named James. One was James, the brother of John the Apostle—both sons of Zebedee; the other was James the son of Alphaeus.) In fact, it appears from Scripture that James *the younger* had not become a believer in Jesus until after His resurrection.[3] As a result, he had to learn from others the lessons Jesus had taught.

While James had not been present at the Last Supper when Jesus gave the New Commandment, he was one of the 120 that gathered in an upper room after Jesus' ascension. As instructed by Jesus, they were waiting for the promised Holy Spirit that would guide, teach, and empower the new believers. No doubt, he heard the apostles that were in the room talking about the New Covenant and the Command that Jesus had given them at the Last Supper. James would also have experienced the

---

[1] James 1:1b
[2] Mark 15:40
[3] See Matthew 13:55, Mark 6:3

heavenly culture of love for one another that was so clearly demonstrated in the church of Jerusalem in those early years.

With the passage of time, James found himself as the recognized leader of this growing congregation in Jerusalem. He had no New Testament Scriptures to rely on, no written gospel account or letters with John's description of the Command Jesus had given. Yet James knew that there was now a law that fulfilled and superseded the Law of Moses.

As James wrote what would become the first New Testament Scripture, he reached back into the only Scriptures available to him, the Torah, and chose one command from the Book of Leviticus on which to base the new law that was now governing them. The small phrase he chose seemed rather obscure, found only one time in Old Testament Scriptures. Nevertheless, it was well known in that day.

love your neighbor as yourself.[1]

Because most of us live in a secular society, we immediately assume that the "neighbor" they were commanded to love was like our neighbors, possibly an agnostic, an atheist or a person of another religious faith. However, that was not at all the case. They were family, all descendants of Jacob—the man God renamed Israel. His twelve sons became twelve large family units. Known as Israelites, they were brothers and sisters, relatives, a tribal people. They were all members of God's covenant community.

Therefore, their neighbor was their brother, family in both the genealogical and religious sense. Because of this, when God commanded them to "love your neighbor as yourself," He was telling them to "love one another!" This becomes clear when looking at the context of these words as found in Leviticus.

---

[1] Leviticus 19:18b

> 16   "'Do not go about spreading slander among *your people*. "'Do not do anything that endangers *your neighbor's* life. I am the LORD.
> 17   "'Do not hate *your brother* in your heart. Rebuke *your neighbor* frankly so you will not share in his guilt.
> 18   "'Do not seek revenge or bear a grudge against one of *your people*, but love *your neighbor* as yourself. I am the LORD.[1]

You can hear the rhythmic use of "your people/your neighbor," and "your brother/your neighbor." Their neighbor was their brother, their people. Indeed, they were being commanded to *love one another*.

James seized on this phrase from the Law of Moses and brought it forward for the first time into the New Covenant and the life of the primitive Christian church.

> If you really keep the royal law found in Scripture, "Love your neighbor as yourself," you are doing right.[2]

As we have just seen from Israel's history, "love your neighbor as yourself" was the closest equivalent that could be found to "love one another"—the command that Jesus gave us and the phrase that would later be written many times in New Testament Scripture.

Yet even as James reached back into the Torah for this commandment, he knew that it was different—*new*—exceeding all that had gone before. To distinguish the new from the old, he gives it a new title, the "King's Law."

---

[1] Excerpts from Leviticus 19:16-18
[2] James 2:8

While usually rendered the "royal law," I believe it would have been better translated the King's Law[1] because the word "royal"—*basilikon* in Greek—actually means "belonging to a king."[2] In giving it the title the King's Law, James elevates it to a place that is higher than the Law of Moses. Moses was not a king but now the Kingdom of Heaven was coming and the King had given His Commandment. It would be the "law of the land" for all of those in His domain.

James has already laid the foundation of this when earlier in his letter he refers to this new law as "the perfect law that gives freedom . . ."[3]

> But the man who looks intently into *the perfect law that gives freedom*, and continues to do this, not forgetting what he has heard, but doing it—he will be blessed in what he does.[4]

For James, this was expressed as the King's Law, *loving your neighbor as yourself — loving one another*—and for those that lived according to it, there was freedom and blessing. He goes on to urge those that were "believers in our glorious Lord Jesus Christ"[5] not to favor the rich or dishonor the poor that were part of their fellowship, because to do so would not be in keeping with the King's Law. Rather, they were to conduct themselves in keeping with the perfect law that gave freedom.

> Speak and act as those who are going to be judged by *the law that gives freedom*, because judgment without

---

[1] "Theologically important is James 2:8 . . ." "It signifies the law as given by the (King)." ". . . it is better to give it the more specific sense and . . . to see in it a reference to God as the (King) who makes law." (Kittel's, *Theological Dictionary of the New Testament*)
[2] See Acts 12:20 as an example of this use of the word
[3] James 1:25
[4] James 1:25
[5] James 2:1a

mercy will be shown to anyone who has not been merciful. Mercy triumphs over judgment![1]

Again, James referred to this new kind of law, a law that gives freedom. He contrasts the law that gives freedom with what he called the whole law, meaning that law which was given to Moses and governed the former covenant. In large part, it was a law that lacked the provision of mercy. James reminded them of the absence of mercy when he wrote, "whoever keeps the whole law and yet stumbles at just one point is guilty of breaking all of it."[2] Apparently, in James' experience, the Law of Moses was not a perfect law that gave freedom!

In my understanding, this would have been James' early teaching about the Command of Christ to "the twelve tribes scattered among the nations" as well as to the Jerusalem church he pastored. A new law had been introduced, not one that diminished the whole law but rather one that superseded it. It was the *King's Law*. In reality, it was the *Law of Christ*.

About thirty years after James wrote his letter citing the *King's Law,* John would write what we know as the Gospel of John, that part of the Scripture in which we find "For God so loved the world, that he gave his only begotten Son"[3] and "A new command I give you: Love one another."[4] John's writings and first hand account of Jesus' teaching and interaction with the disciples would give us crucial insight, filling in some of the details not included in the Gospel accounts written by Matthew, Mark, and Luke.

James was not the only one that was writing New Covenant Scripture without the benefit of Jesus' Command in written

---

[1] James 2:12, 13
[2] James 2:10
[3] John 3:16a King James Version
[4] John 13:34a

form. Because John's writings were the last to be completed, none of the New Testament writers had the benefit of John's account of the Command. That makes it all the more significant that we find the words *love one another* or their near equivalent over twenty times in the New Testament letters.

In writing to the new followers of Jesus, James knew that those who had lived under the Law given by Moses had to know *the perfect law, the law that gives freedom, the King's Law!* They were living in a New Covenant with a New Law. The King's Law contained the One Commandment Jesus gave us, to love one another as He had loved us.

> If you really keep the royal law found in Scripture, "Love your neighbor as yourself," *you are doing right.*[1]

James' words "you are doing right" reassure us and affirm a very simple code of conduct for believers in the New Covenant. When you love one another, you are doing what God desires of you. It is indeed a very simple code of conduct, but one that fulfills the Law given in the previous covenant. It is the King's Law.

As I'm writing this part of the book, my wife and I are staying in a home in the beautiful city of Piedmont, California. We can look out of the front window and see the entire Bay Area including the city of San Francisco and the Golden Gate Bridge.

---

[1] James 2:8

I'm an early riser. Early each morning, I've been driving down the narrow winding streets to the picturesque Montclair Village to gain internet access and to continue my writing.

Parking is at a premium in Montclair Village and the meter eagerly gobbles up ten quarters for the two-hour maximum. A couple of mornings ago, I fed the parking meter, duly noting the time and then had a very productive time of writing. I was keeping an eye on my watch as the two hours of metered time was ending. When the time was almost up, I stepped out of the café only to see a police officer standing next to my car. I was shocked to think that it had expired and quickly took about a dozen steps to where he was standing. I arrived just in time to hear the faint whirring sound of the little computerized ticket-writer he held in his hand. It spit out a parking violation--$35.

I wanted to plead for mercy. I had paid the full price for the two hours. It seemed impossible that I could have been more than thirty seconds over the allotted time. It's possible that at first glance he noticed that the time was so close to expiring that he paused, took a deep breath of morning air and then pushed the button on his little ticket writer as the word "expired" popped up. It had to have been that close!

There was no point in arguing the fact. I had kept the law for 120 minutes but at 121 minutes, I was as guilty as if I had parked all two hours without filling the meter. I meekly took the ticket from his hand and managed a weak "Thank you."

The rest of the day was not the same. I felt paranoid, braking sharply when I noticed the front edge of my bumper going slightly into the wide white line at a pedestrian crossing. I reflexively jerked the steering wheel to the left when I saw the front wheel of a parked car pointed into my lane—only to realize no one was in the car. A sense of dread hung over me for the rest of that day and into the next. It seemed that I was constantly breaking the law. I felt no freedom. The "law" seemed to loom over me. In fact, my focus was no longer on driving safely; it was now on the law and on the paranoia that came from seeing how often I seemed to be breaking it!

I'm not saying that the law is "bad" or "wrong." What I am saying is that the law is typically not known for creating freedom. Yet James saw that the King's Law was a perfect law, a law that gave freedom.

I think that is what Jesus had in mind when He said "For my yoke is easy and my burden is light"[1] and "My command is this: Love each other as I have loved you."[2] He had come to set us free from slavery to sin and the law that gave sin authority over us. He had told them "if the Son sets you free, you will be free indeed."[3]

Paul had also seen this freedom as a prime feature of the New Covenant, one he was unwilling to compromise.

> It is for freedom that Christ has set us free. Stand firm, then, and do not let yourselves be burdened again by a yoke of slavery. Mark my words! I, Paul, tell you that if you let yourselves be circumcised, Christ will be of no value to you at all. Again I declare to every man who lets himself be circumcised that he is obligated to obey *the whole law*.[4]

Clearly, living under *the whole law*[5] was not the freedom experienced by those that now embraced the King's Law!

---

[1] Matthew 11:30
[2] John 15:12
[3] John 8:36
[4] Galatians 5:1-3
[5] See Matthew 22:40, Galatians 5:3 and James 2:10

CHAPTER 15

THE LAW OF CHRIST

One of the early steps in my personal journey of discovery was to see the connection between Jesus' One Commandment and the Law of Christ. Paul introduces us to the Law of Christ in the first letter he wrote, his letter to the believers in Galatia.

> Carry each other's burdens, and in this way you will fulfill the *Law of Christ*.[1]

As with the letter written by James, it is important to recognize that Paul also is writing thirty years before John would write Jesus' actual words, "My command is this: Love each other as I have loved you."[2] Again, it is worth noting that Paul was not one of the twelve who listened to Jesus' teachings for three years. Therefore, Paul's introduction of the phrase "Law of Christ" is extremely insightful and no doubt came as one of the special revelations he received from God.

The instruction given by Paul in his Galatian letter helped me in a number of ways. First, it helped me by simply introducing the words Law of Christ. I had been more familiar with the Law of Moses than I was the Law of Christ. I knew that the Law of Moses contained the Ten Commandments so whenever I came across the word *law* in my study of the New Testament, I automatically assumed it was a reference to the Law of Moses. Now for the first time, I recognized that there was another option, the Law of Christ. It contained the One Commandment. That gave new meaning to some of the uses of the word *law* in

---

[1] Galatians 6:2
[2] John 15:12

the New Testament. There were clearly times that *law* was referring to the Law of Christ rather than the Law of Moses.

Second, Paul's introduction of the Law of Christ helped me understand what Jesus' Command looks like in practical terms. When I help one of my brothers or sisters carry their excessively heavy burden, I am obeying the Command and fulfilling the Law of Christ. Nearly all of us experience a crushing burden at some point in our lives. It's the kind of load that would "tip your wagon over" if someone did not come to give you aid in that moment.

John the apostle writes in 1 John 3:16, "This is how we know what love is: Jesus Christ laid down his life for us. And we ought to lay down our lives for our brothers."[1] 1 John 3:16 is the less known "John 3:16." Nevertheless, it is an important part of authentic Christian discipleship and we would do well to link it with the more familiar John 3:16, "For God so loved the world that he gave his one and only Son, that whoever believes in him shall not perish but have eternal life."[2]

No doubt, there is a direct link between "carrying each other's burdens" and the words written immediately before it.

> Brothers, if someone is caught in a sin, you who are spiritual should restore him gently. But watch yourself, or you also may be tempted. Carry each other's burdens, and in this way you will fulfill the Law of Christ.[3]

---

[1] 1 John 3:16
[2] John 3:16
[3] Galatians 6:1, 2

The excessive burden[1] referred to in this sentence could very likely be a character flaw or some personal weakness in a sister or brother's life that has made them vulnerable to a particular sin. This vulnerability has contributed to their being caught or ensnared by sin. The Law of Christ, with its One Command to love one another, would move us toward this friend in need rather than away from them in their moment of difficulty. It would motivate us to restore them. The Command of Christ would make us gentle in our life-giving effort. It would also motivate us to act with humility rather than judgment, recognizing that we are not immune to similar temptations.

When I obey the Command of Christ, I am moved with compassion to put a shoulder under the excessive burden of a brother or sister in need. When I help them, I fulfill the Law of Christ.

It is clear that Paul's reference to the Law of Christ was more than a passing fancy from his use of it a second time. This time he is writing his first letter to the church at Corinth.

I . . . am under *Christ's law*[2]

Paul writes this in the context of his compelling passion to preach the Good News about Jesus Christ to people wherever he went. He had a strong desire to influence as many as possible to put their faith in the Savior. Again, here it is in his words.

---

[1] In some translations, the word "burden" is found again in verse five; "For every man shall bear his own burden." Galatians 6:5 (KJV) The word "burden," found here in the KJV is a completely different word than the one used in verse two just moments earlier. The word "burden" in verse five is related to the "invoice" or "manifest" which lists the cargo carried in a sailing vessel or ship. That "burden" is the part of daily living which is really yours to carry and you can carry it. The word "burden," as used earlier in verse two, is "the excessive load."

[2] 1 Corinthians 9:21b

> Though I am free and belong to no man, I make myself
> a slave to everyone, to win as many as possible. To the
> Jews I became like a Jew, to win the Jews. To those
> under the law I became like one under the law (though I
> myself am not under the law), so as to win those under
> the law. To those not having the law I became like one
> not having the law (though I am not free from God's
> law but am under *Christ's law*), so as to win those not
> having the law. To the weak I became weak, to win the
> weak. I have become all things to all men so that by all
> possible means I might save some.[1]

For me, Paul's train of thought is a bit difficult to follow, yet
very significant. Because of my quest to understand the
Command of Christ, I was immediately drawn to his reference
to *Christ's law*. I was struck by how real the *Law of Christ* was
to Paul.

From his life experience before conversion to faith in Jesus,
Paul knew what it was to live under the law given to Moses. He
describes his past spirituality as "a Hebrew of Hebrews; in
regard to the law, a Pharisee . . . [and] as for legalistic
righteousness, faultless."[2]

While he was willing to identify with those now living under the
Law of Moses, Paul knew that he no longer lived at that address.
However, he was willing to go to that address to win someone
who still lived there.

> to win those under the law . . . I became like one under
> the law (though I myself am not under the law)[3]

---

[1] 1 Corinthians 9:19-22
[2] Philippians 3:5b, 6b
[3] 1 Corinthians 9:20c, b

In the Greek language, *under the law* was *hupo (under) nomos (law)*. Again, Paul had lived hupo nomos (under the law) but didn't live there any longer.

Additionally, Paul wanted to win "pagans," people who knew nothing about the Law of Moses. Here's how he says it.

> to win those not having the law[1] . . . I became like one not having the law[2]

Here, Paul combines two Greek words for "not having the law"—*a (without)* and *nomos (law)—anomos*. You could think of it somewhat like our use of the words *amoral* and *moral*.

But Paul didn't live here either. He was not *under the law (hupo nomos)* and yet he was not *without law (anomos)*. However, that didn't make him free from God's law. Here is how he put it.

> I am not free from God's law but am *under Christ's law*[3]

Paul was very aware that while he was *not under the Law of Moses,* he was *not free from God's Law—a lawless man.* He knew there was another alternative—*the Law of Christ!* The Law of Christ was now God's Law for Paul and that was his "current address!" Living there was so important to Paul that he was willing to go to any length to see people everywhere join him. He wanted to win them to Jesus, the Messiah.

Before we leave these words, there is one more point to consider. From reading most Bible translations of this verse, we would be left with the impression that while Paul no longer lived "*under (hupo)* the Law" of Moses, he now lived "*under*

---

[1] 1 Corinthians 9:21d,
[2] 1 Corinthians 9:21b
[3] 1 Corinthians 9:21b

(hupo) the Law of Christ." However, that is not what he wrote in the Greek language. Rather, he introduced another word, "ennomos," to describe where he now lived. Literally, Paul is saying that he now lived *"in the Law of Christ."*

Does that make a difference? Apparently, Paul thought it did. Living "under" something implies weight or heaviness. Living "in" something implies abiding, shelter, protection, being at home or at rest. Strong strengthens this thought when he describes this word *en* as a "position" or "state" and then adds "i.e. a relation of rest."[1] I believe this is what Paul called "living the life of love."[2] It was a lifestyle of keeping the Command of Christ—to love one another as He had loved us.

It seems to me that most of us don't have anywhere near the clarity that Paul had about his position in relationship to God's Law. As a Pharisee of the Pharisees, he had lived much of his life *under the Law (hupo nomos)* but that was no longer his home. He now lived *in the Law of Christ (ennomos Christou).*

According to Paul, the whole Law was fulfilled when they obeyed Jesus' Command to love one another. He points this out to the Galatians in the same letter in which he introduced the Law of Christ.

> You, my brothers, were called to be free. But do not use your freedom to indulge the sinful nature; rather, *serve one another in love.* The entire law is summed up in a single command: "Love your neighbor as yourself."[3]

---

[1] "en; a primary preposition denoting (fixed) position (in place, time or state), and (by implication) instrumentality . . . , i.e. a relation of rest . . . ." (Strong's New Exhaustive Concordance)
[2] Ephesians 5:2
[3] Galatians 5:13-14

Even as James drew a sentence from the Torah—calling it the King's Law, Paul too uses this same Scriptural quotation—"Love your neighbor as yourself"—as being the equivalent of "love one another." In saying that the "entire law is summed up in a single command," Paul is agreeing with the One Command Jesus gave. He reiterates this truth in his most systematic teaching of all, his letter to the Romans.

> Let no debt remain outstanding, except the continuing debt *to love one another*, for *he who loves [another] has fulfilled the law*. The commandments, "Do not commit adultery," "Do not murder," "Do not steal," "Do not covet," and whatever other commandment there may be, are summed up in this one rule: "Love your neighbor as yourself." Love does no harm to its neighbor. Therefore love is the fulfillment of the law."[1]

To Paul, the Law of Christ was the law of love. Living in the Law of Christ was simply living a life of love. I believe this is what Paul had in mind when he wrote, "Therefore, as we have opportunity, let us do good to all people, especially to those who belong to the family of believers."[2]

---

[1] Romans 13:8-10
[2] Galatians 6:10

CHAPTER 16

LOVE COVERS—LOVE CONFRONTS

In my personal journey of discovering the Law of Christ, I've had to take a new look at words of Scripture that were already very familiar to me. One of those was in the writings of Peter, the first disciple of Jesus and a leader among the twelve apostles.

> Above all, love each other deeply, because love covers over a multitude of sins.[1]

From reading the Gospels, I remember Peter as a crusty, opinionated, outspoken, arrogant, sword-swinging fisherman from the region of Galilee. He was a man's man. It seemed that he never lacked the courage to say what he was thinking and appeared to have a rather high opinion of himself. He certainly didn't seem like the kind of man that went around passing out flowers to people and talking about *love* all the time.

However, this is Peter some thirty years later, now a seasoned apostle who is writing his first letter. He's saying things like "Now that you have purified yourselves by obeying the truth so that you have sincere love for your brothers, love one another deeply, from the heart. For you have been born again"[2]

From my previous vantage point, I wouldn't have seen these words as tied to the Jesus' Command. Now it is unmistakable. Peter was at the Passover meal that historic night that Jesus "took bread and broke it, saying 'This is my body given for you;

---

[1] 1 Peter 4:8
[2] 1 Peter 1:22, 23a

do this in remembrance of me'." Then after the supper, He "took the cup, saying, 'This cup is the new covenant in my blood, which is poured out for you'."[1]

But Peter seemed a bit distracted when minutes later Jesus said, "A new command I give you: Love one another. As I have loved you, so you must love one another."[2] I say "distracted" because immediately before introducing the New Command, Jesus had told them that He would be leaving them soon and they wouldn't be able to go with Him.[3]

Peter was used to going places with Jesus. In fact, he was invited to go places that other disciples didn't get to go. It didn't seem to set very well with him that he was not being given a special invitation to go with Jesus on this journey. Peter's immediate words *after* Jesus gave the New Commandment had nothing to with what Jesus had just said. He was "stuck" on Jesus' leaving without him.

Fortunately, Jesus repeated the Command two more times before the evening was over, now owning it as "My Command." Apparently, Peter got it. Now thirty years later, he writes the Command twice in his first letter.

> Now that you have purified yourselves by obeying the truth so that you have *sincere love for your brothers,* *love one another deeply, from the heart.*[4]

> Above all, *love each other deeply*, because *love covers* over a multitude of sins.[5]

---

[1] Luke 22:19b, 20a
[2] John 13:34
[3] See John 13:33-36
[4] 1 Peter 1:22
[5] 1 Peter 4:8

What I noticed is that Peter surrounds the Command in these two accounts with words like *above, all, deeply,* and *from the heart.* These words, when used individually, are very powerful but when they are combined around one thought—*love one another*—have an exponential power with even more expansive implications.

What's unique about how Peter "got it" is the thought that he attaches to *loving one another.*

because love *covers over a multitude of sins.*[1]

I think Peter understood the importance of *love covering a multitude of sins* from his own personal experience. That lesson was gleaned from two of the longest nights that Peter had ever lived through.

The first was the night of the Last Supper. Jesus introduced the New Covenant during the meal as He broke the bread then took the cup. After the Passover meal was over, He washed His disciples' feet as an example of His love and a model of servant leadership. He then told them that He would be leaving and gave them the New Commandment.

Then Jesus took them to pray with Him in the garden of Gethsemane. As Jesus now confronts what lies ahead, His agony is palpable, three times alternating between prayers which seek some other alternative and surrender to His Father's will. Then came the moment of His betrayal and arrest. Of course, Peter took a couple of swings with his sword—netting one ear in the process.[2]

After His arrest, authorities questioned Jesus. Peter had chosen to follow at a distance to see the outcome. It was a cold night

---

[1] 1 Peter 4:8b
[2] See John 18:10

and he blended into a mixed crowd of servants, soldiers and the curious who were warming themselves around an open fire in the courtyard. Suddenly, a young servant girl pointed at Peter and spoke.

> "You also were with Jesus of Galilee," she said. But he denied it before them all. "I don't know what you're talking about," he said. Then he went out to the gateway, where another girl saw him and said to the people there, "This fellow was with Jesus of Nazareth." He denied it again, with an oath: "I don't know the man!" After a little while, those standing there went up to Peter and said, "Surely you are one of them, for your accent gives you away." Then he began to call down curses on himself and he swore to them, "I don't know the man!" Immediately a rooster crowed.[1]

What made this all the more painful was Peter's bold response when just hours earlier, Jesus had predicted that all of them would abandon Him that night.

> Peter replied, "Even if all fall away on account of you, I never will."[2]

> "I tell you the truth," Jesus answered, "this very night, before the rooster crows, you will disown me three times."[3]

> But Peter declared, "Even if I have to die with you, I will never disown you."[4]

---

[1] Matthew 26:69b-74
[2] Matthew 26:33
[3] Matthew 26:34
[4] Matthew 26:35a

For Peter, I'm sure what was happening now was like a nightmare that wouldn't end.

> The Lord turned and looked straight at Peter. Then Peter remembered the word the Lord had spoken to him: "Before the rooster crows today, you will disown me three times." And he went outside and wept bitterly.[1]

I think that the agony Peter was experiencing that long night goes way beyond description. The next day Jesus was crucified. Then there were the days that they spent behind locked doors in the grip of fear, uncertainty, and numbing doubt. They were no heroes at that moment in history, simply men struggling with their doubts and fears.

Yes, it must have helped greatly when the resurrected Jesus appeared to ten of the disciples later that evening as they were huddled behind locked doors. I'm sure it helped when Jesus, a week later, made a special visit to allay the doubts of Thomas who had been absent when He first visited the soon-to-be apostles.

That first long night had ended weeks earlier but I have a sense that the guilt that engulfed Peter lingered on. I don't think he could forget his shameful behavior, the unbelievable cowardice he had displayed on that night of nights. In my opinion, Peter thought it was over for him. He had disqualified himself. His future was fishing on Lake Galilee.

For that reason, I think it was Jesus' third appearance to the disciples that was most significant for Peter. I believe it impacted Peter so deeply that he was thinking of it thirty years

---

[1] Luke 22:61, 62

later when he wrote, "Above all, love each other deeply, because love covers over a multitude of sins."[1]

Here's the story surrounding that third appearance. Peter and some of the other disciples had decided to get out of Jerusalem after the mix of devastating and perplexing experiences that accompanied the arrest, crucifixion and resurrection of Jesus, their promised Messiah. Peter and six other disciples were together in one of the small villages on the shore of Galilee when Peter announced that he was going fishing.

Peter was a leader. The six others that were present—including John—decided immediately to go with Peter. It was probably late afternoon when they got into the boat. A night of hard work on the lake had failed to net even one small fish. It seemed that they were ready to "throw in the towel" as morning neared. They were still about the length of a football field[2] from the shore and the night sky was just starting to get its first tones of grey when they heard a voice coming across the water. Here is where it gets interesting.

Friends, haven't you any fish?[3]

"No," they answered.[4]

Throw your net on the right side of the boat and you will find some.[5]

When they did, they were unable to haul the net in because of the large number of fish. Then [John] . . . said to Peter, "It is the Lord!" As soon as Simon Peter

---

[1] 1 Peter 4:8
[2] a hundred yards; See John 21:8 NIV
[3] John 21:5b
[4] John 21:5c
[5] John 21:6a

heard him say, "It is the Lord," he wrapped his outer garment around him (for he had taken it off) and jumped into the water. The other disciples followed in the boat, towing the net full of fish . . . [1]

As Peter climbed ashore, he could no doubt smell breakfast cooking. Fish were frying on the glowing coals. Bread was standing ready. The first words exchanged were Jesus asking Peter to bring a few more fish from their recent catch to add to the breakfast that He was cooking.

At that request, it appears that Peter is back in charge—on the boat getting the catch onto the shore. Apparently it seemed important that they take time to count the fish—one hundred fifty three—and examine the quality of the catch as well—large fish. They also noted that the net had not been torn in spite of the astonishing size of the catch.

Then Jesus announced that breakfast was ready and again took the role of servant as He gave the fish and bread to the seven hungry fishermen. It appears that the silence was awkward and the setting somewhat surreal as they ate together. While they knew that it was the Lord, they still had the inner urge to inquire.[2] Nevertheless, no one could muster up the courage to make the inquiry and the question went unasked as they munched on the breakfast that Jesus had prepared for them.[3]

When they had their fill of fish and bread, Jesus turned His attention to only one of the seven fishermen present—Peter. It would now become clear that for all practical purposes this meeting was about him and him alone.

---

[1] John 21:6b, 7a, c, 8a
[2] See John 21:12
[3] Read this part of the story in John 21:9-14

When they had finished eating, Jesus said to Simon Peter, "Simon son of John, do you truly love me more than these?"[1]

As He asked this question, Jesus may well have fixed His gaze on a net brimming with the largest catch that had ever been taken from the Sea of Galilee. It had been three years since Jesus had first called to Simon Peter as he was fishing with his father on this very lake.[2] Once again, Simon Peter is fishing and Jesus is calling him from his first love for the second time.

"Yes, Lord," he said, "you know that I love you."

"Feed my lambs."

Again Jesus said, "Simon son of John, do you truly love me?"

"Yes, Lord, you know that I love you."

"Take care of my sheep."

The third time he said to him, "Simon son of John, do you love me?"

Peter was hurt because Jesus asked him the third time, "Do you love me?" He said, "Lord, you know all things; you know that I love you."

"Feed my sheep.[3]

Life has a lot to do with competing loves. If our first love is success in any field of endeavor rather than love for God, His

---

[1] John 21:15
[2] See Matthew 4:18-20
[3] Excerpts from John 21:15-17

call to us will be to personal obedience that comes from a motivation of love—love for Him.

In Peter's case, love for Jesus would be expressed by feeding the sheep—loving people, Jesus' sheep, as He had commanded. That's really the call for all of us. "If you love me, obey me. Obey what I command you. My command is that you love each other."

This second long night for Peter was ending. In the first long night, he had denied Jesus three times as he warmed himself by a fire. In this second long night, Jesus had confronted Peter's waffling and had led him to profess his love for Him three times by the warmth of another fire, a fire that had been kindled by a true friend.

Only weeks later, Peter would stand with the other apostles and preach his first sermon. He would boldly declare that "this is what was spoken by the prophet Joel: "'In the last days, God says, I will pour out my Spirit on all people'."[1] Three thousand people would step out of the crowd and become followers of the risen Lord Jesus—the one that had so recently fixed breakfast on the shore for Peter and his "fisherman" friends.

Once again, we look at the words that Peter writes thirty years after he had endured two very long nights.

> Above all, love each other deeply, because love covers over a multitude of sins.[2]

I think Peter really believed that he was disqualified by his shameful denial of his Master and Teacher. He didn't deserve to be called a disciple of Jesus Christ. What's more, the thought of

---

[1] Acts 2:16b, 17a
[2] 1 Peter 4:8

being an apostle was no longer in Peter's picture of his future. But then Jesus confronted him.

What about me? What about you? How many of us would be disqualified if someone hadn't loved us enough to pursue us in our darkest moment?

While it is true that love covers, love is not a cover-up. Love does cover, but it also confronts. Love that confronts doesn't always look the way I may have pictured it or practiced it. In my mind, confrontation has always been something like, "Meet me in my office at 3:15 this afternoon!" or knocking on someone's door and announcing, "I'm here on the basis of Matthew 18 to talk to you about your sin."

When confronting sin in ourselves or in others, it is important to remember God's amazing qualities of kindness, tolerance, and patience. We should never treat these qualities as insignificant or with contempt.

> Or do you show contempt for the riches of his kindness, tolerance and patience, not realizing that God's kindness leads you toward repentance?[1]

Certainly, Jesus' kindness had gotten to Peter that morning. He would never forget the Command that Jesus had given them and the miracle of that life-changing moment on the shore of the lake where again he heard the words of his Lord: "Follow me!"

---

[1] Romans 2:4

CHAPTER 17

DO I LOVE'EM OR HATE'EM?

From what I see in the Bible, there must be a very fine line between *love* and *hate*. For instance, in the Ten Commandments God had promised to "punish the children for the sin of the fathers to the third and fourth generation of those that *hate me*, but show love to a thousand generations of those who *love me* and keep my commandments."[1] As I read those words, it seemed that God didn't leave any "middle ground" of indifference between *love* and *hate*. You either love God or hate Him.

This truth seemed unchanged in the New Testament. In John the Apostle's first letter, he uses *love* and *hate* in the same way, again giving no "middle ground" between the two. He writes, "Anyone who claims to be in the light but *hates* his brother is still in the darkness. Whoever *loves* his brother lives in the light, and there is nothing in him to make him stumble."[2]

John continues.

> If someone says, "I *love* God," and *hates* his brother, he is a liar; for the one who does *not love* his brother whom he has seen, cannot *love* God whom he has not seen.[3]

I really don't like it that way. I would prefer a large mushy-middle-ground between *love* and *hate*, a place where I could live

---

[1] Exodus 20:5b, 6
[2] 1 John 2:9-10
[3] 1 John 4:20

most of the time. From this mushy terrain of indifference, I could proclaim in self-defense, "I may not *love 'em*, but I *for sure* don't *hate 'em!"*

However, the words "anyone who does not love his brother" imply that anything less than love falls across the line into the category of hate. This understanding is supported by Strong when in defining the word *hate (miseo* in Greek*)* he states that one of the meanings of hate is "to love less."[1] In other words, hate can be defined as anything less than love or anything loved less. Where love stops, hate starts. The large mushy-middle-ground that I would plead for does not seem to exist from God's perspective.

One day when my wife's Pontiac Bonneville was being serviced, she asked to use my Chevy Metro. My car has a three-cylinder engine that produces a whopping fifty-five horsepower, a stick shift and lacks most of the power accessories that we are accustomed to these days. When she brought my car back later in the day, her first comment as she walked through the door was "I hate your car!" My response to her was, "You didn't have to drive it. You could have walked!" to which she countered, "Well, I don't really *hate* your car; I just like it a lot *less* than I like my Pontiac!"

In the Scriptural sense of love and hate, she was probably right both times. Because of her "like it less" feeling toward my car, she really did hate it in the Biblical language! She loved her Bonneville and hated my Metro!

If Scriptural hate is anything less than love, hate is a continuum that starts with indifference and extends all the way to murder on the extreme end. Everything in this continuum of hate is based on selfishness, "me first" all the way to "me only"

---

[1] James Strong, *Strong's Exhaustive Concordance of the Bible*

without you on the planet. While indifference seems much more benign than murder, it leans towards murder from the start.

This theme of love and hate started very early in the record of Scripture. The importance of this topic is revealed by the first question God asks. It is a simple question directed to Adam and Eve.

Where are you?[1]

They were hiding. The thought of a late afternoon stroll with God through the garden struck fear in them—something they had never experienced before. God had given them one command.

You are free to eat from any tree in the garden; but you must not eat from the tree of the knowledge of good and evil,[2]

There were "a thousand trees"[3] in the garden from which God said they could eat. However, they chose the *one* tree from which He had instructed them *not* to eat! Suddenly, they seemed exposed—uncovered, ashamed for the first time.

The reason God asked them the question—"Where are you?"— is not because He had lost track of the man and woman He had created. Rather, the question was asked because they needed to find themselves! They needed to realize what they had done and where their choice had led them. They needed to understand that their trust in God had been broken. Consequently, they were now doing their very best to hide from Him. Loving relationship between the Creator and His creation had been interrupted.

---

[1] Genesis 3:9b
[2] Genesis 2:16b, 17a
[3] My figure of speech

The second question we hear God asking is directed to one of Adam and Eve's sons.

Where is your brother Abel?[1]

The reason for this question is that relationship between two brothers had been broken—badly broken! Actually, Cain had just killed his brother, Abel. Again, God is not asking this question because He doesn't know where to find Abel. He had already heard Abel's blood crying from the ground. Rather, God asks the question to expose Cain's flawed thinking and immoral conduct.

I think these two questions correspond to the two core commandments of both the Old and New covenants. We should all take these two questions to heart. "Where are you?" is God's question to us about the nature of our relationship with Him. "Where is your brother?" is God's question to us about the nature of our relationship with one another.

In the Christian faith, we understand that our relationship with God is restored when we place our faith in His Son, Jesus Christ. Our relationship with one another is restored when we love one another as Jesus commanded us. These are the *two core commandments* of Christian discipleship as taught in New Testament Scripture.

I find the first question Cain asked God to be indicative of the greatest problem we face in our relationship with one another!

Am I my brother's keeper?[2]

We see that Cain's self-absorbed attitude moved quickly from *indifference* toward his brother to actually *murdering* him. No

---

[1] Genesis 4:9b
[2] Genesis 4:9a

wonder we see the following words in New Testament Scripture.

> This is how we know who the children of God are and who the children of the devil are: Anyone who does not do what is right is not a child of God; nor is anyone who does not love his brother. This is the message you heard from the beginning: We should *love one another*. Do not be like Cain, who belonged to the evil one and murdered his brother.[1]

I had begun to see that hate was a continuum that started with apathy or indifference and continued all the way to murder. I gained more insight when a group of pastors in our city started meeting to learn how to love one another. Dave, one of my pastor friends, gave me the second and more important half of the picture. He pointed out that love also was a continuum that started with concern!

This has become an extremely significant insight for me. If hate is a continuum that starts with indifference, love starts with concern and extends all the way to giving your life so another can live. That understanding allowed me to see why I could find no "mushy-middle-ground" between love and hate; there wasn't any! Concern stands right next to indifference but they lean in opposite directions. Just as indifference leans towards murder, so concern leans toward laying one's life down for another.

---

[1] 1 John 3: 10-12

Love and Hate

Love | Hate

vs.

Love | mushy-middle-ground | Hate

Love Continuum | Hate Continuum

Dying for another <-----Concern | Indifference ------------ > Murder

As pastors in our city continued to meet and build loving relationships, I saw the Scriptural basis for the thought my friend Dave had brought to the table. This theme of *concern* is found in the prelude to Paul's well-known teaching about love in 1 Corinthians 13. There Paul introduces the theme by comparing our relationship with one another to the parts of a human body. For one part of the body to say it has no need of the other parts is unimaginable. He puts it this way.

> And the eye cannot say to the hand, "I have no need of you"; nor again the head to the feet, "I have no need of you."[1]

Rather than living as if we don't need each other, Paul says that we should have "equal *concern* for one another." In my understanding, this *concern* is the place we have been talking about, the place where love starts.

> God has combined the members of the body and has given greater honor to the parts that lacked it, so that

---

[1] 1 Corinthians 12:21 New King James Version

there should be no division in the body, but that its parts should have equal *concern* for each other.[1]

Paul sees this equal concern as the secret to being united, the way we keep from being divided from one another. I believe that Christian unity is never achieved when unity is the end for which we seek. Attempts at unity inevitably fail when they are approached in this manner. Rather, unity is the direct result of us loving one another. It is a gift God gives us and we are to guard it by our obedience to Jesus' Command—"love one another as I have loved you."

Only His kind of selfless love can motivate us to begin this journey of love, to be concerned for another part of the body. Love, starting with genuine concern for one another, will guard against breaking the unity of the Spirit. Love is the antidote for division among believers. The best way to guard that precious gift of unity is to obey the Command that Jesus gave us.

With that in mind, I took another look at what John had written.

> "We love because he first loved us. If anyone says, "I love God," yet hates his brother, he is a liar. For anyone who does not love his brother, whom he has seen, *cannot* love God, whom he has not seen. And he has given us this command: Whoever loves God must also love his brother."[2]

I was struck by the fact that I cannot love God if I am indifferent towards my brothers and sisters. I cannot be a lover of God and fail to keep Jesus' Command to "love one another."

---

[1] 1 Corinthians 12:25
[2] 1 John 4:19-21

As part of my personal journey of discovery, I was reading Adam Clarke's commentary written in the early 1800's on John's account of the Gospel. Clarke was commenting on Jesus' words, "that ye love one another."[1] As part of his commentary, he gives a brief account of a story told by Jerome, the fourth century Christian leader, about John the Apostle.

> "in his extreme old age, when he used to be carried to the public assemblies of the believers, his constant saying was, Little children, love one another. His disciples, wearied at last with the constant repetition of the same words, asked him, Why he constantly said the same thing? 'Because (said he) it is the commandment of the Lord, and the observation of it alone is sufficient.'"[2]

"The commandment of the Lord!" That caught my attention and I began a search to find out more of what Jerome was talking about when he recorded this story. From what Clarke had said, it seemed I would find it in Jerome's commentary on the Galatian letter written by Paul. For the next couple of years, I searched for Jerome's commentary on Galatians. When my travels would take me near major seminary libraries, I would continue my search and ask for help in find it. Surprisingly, no one was able to help me find it.

As I was nearing the end of my writing, the long search came to a successful conclusion one Friday afternoon when the head reference librarian at Loyola Marymount University was

---

[1] Adam Clarke, *Commentary On The New Testament*, Volume 6, (written 1810-1826), AGES, p. 277

[2] Quia praeceptum Domini est, et, si solum fiat, sufficit.

assisting me. He was looking in the Patrologia Latina Database via the internet. Suddenly, I spotted the quote I had been looking for highlighted on the monitor! (That was the good news. The bad news was that it was in Latin. Apparently Jerome's commentary on Galatians has never been translated into English.)

Having found it, I now know a little more about the story as Jerome told it. In writing his commentary on Galatians, Jerome came to the following words Paul had written.

> Therefore, as we have opportunity, let us do good to all people, especially to those who belong to the family of believers.[1]

Jerome then tells of a time when John, whom he calls *the blessed evangelist*, lived in Ephesus.[2] He was very advanced in age and would be carried on the hands of his students to gatherings of believers. Inevitably, he would be asked to greet the people.

It seems that John would not engage in small talk. When asked to speak, he would say one thing; "Children, love one another!"

Growing weary of hearing him say the same thing over and over, the students and brothers that were close to John asked him, "Teacher, when given the opportunity to speak, why do you always say the same thing?"

John gave them the reason in this answer. "Because it is the Lord's command and if only it be done, it is enough!"[3]

---

[1] Galatians 6:10
[2] John the apostle was exiled to the Island of Patmos by Roman emperor Domitian. Shortly after the death of Domitian in 96 A.D., John is believed to have returned to Ephesus where he lived until his death.
[3] Pp. 517-518, S. EUSEBII HIERONYMI STRIDONENSIS PRESBYTERI COMMENTARIORUM IN EPISTOLAM AD GALATAS LIBRI TRES. (C)

Even without this bit of oral history that came through Jerome, we have the actual writings of John with his many references to the Command of Christ. But this story serves to remind us of the significance of the One Command that Jesus gave us.

We need to "guard—to protect by never taking our eyes off" the Lord's Command.

CHAPTER 18

BRIDGE: WORDS I WANT
TO HEAR

There are times in life when we know where we want to go but we need a bridge to get us to our destination. If you are like me, you are committed to living in the Command of Christ. You want obedience to Jesus' Command to become your lifestyle. You are saying, "I have the information; now I want to make the application! How do I get to the place where I can love others as Jesus loved me?"

Living a life of love requires that we have a personal reservoir of love that we can draw from. Beyond that, our reservoir must have a source—a rainfall, a spring, a stream, or a river—that continually replenishes it. It is imperative that we arrive at a place where we know we won't run out of love. Where is that place? How do we get there? Where is "the bridge" that will take us to that desired destination?

I have faced that reality and asked those questions. It was about sixteen years ago that I learned a life-changing lesson in a very personal way. I learned that you couldn't give to others what you don't have yourself. Here's how it happened.

After nearly twenty-four years in full-time pastoral ministry, I realized that I needed to take a sabbatical. That was generally unheard of in the circles I ran in. Usually when pastors got as tired as I felt, they simply resigned from their position and sought another congregation to pastor. I was fortunate to be serving a congregation that loved us dearly. In addition, I was surrounded by a wonderful group of lay elders and a staff that were very supportive of us. They were receptive to the idea of my taking a three-month sabbatical.

When the thought of a sabbatical first came to my mind, I considered arranging a travel itinerary that would allow me to spend time with a number of pastors of large congregations. I would ask them to let me "shadow" them for a couple of weeks. That would enable me to get better at what I was doing—to be a more successful pastor.

That idea faded as thoughts of a sabbatical took shape. In its place came a clear sense that my wife and I were to apply for admission to a short-term discipleship training school. This was a rather improbable place for us to go for several reasons, the first being that I didn't like the sponsoring organization. My resistance was because a number of the most promising young people in my congregation had gone through their program and then vanished into thin air. That didn't set well with me in that I was trying to be successful—to "build" my congregation, not give away my best and brightest.

There were other considerations as well. What would our two teenage children do? What about my wife's reluctance to be in a structured program and the large financial cost of this venture? It seemed unlikely that this was going to happen in spite of the sense I had that it was God's plan for us.

As you have probably guessed, all the pieces came together and in a matter of months, we were thousands of miles from our home and enrolled in the program. As it turned out, it would be nearly six months before we would return to our home, family, and pastoral duties.

Our first week in the program was nearly disastrous. We were seasoned adults; being told where we were going to live, what we were going to eat, and what our work duties would be, felt like a total loss of control. Besides that, we didn't have a car—the ultimate means that many of us in the western world use to escape unpleasant circumstances. It was a huge shock to our sensibilities.

There was also the classroom time and small group activities that we were required to attend five days a week. There were sixty of us in the class. Our ages ranged from twenty-eight to seventy-three years. We were from thirteen different countries.

At the heart of the program was a guest lecturer who spoke to us for two hours each day for a week. The lectures were held in a large modern classroom. While some of the students scrambled for the front seats, I chose to sit at the very back of the classroom. My wife, Patti, was at my side. The first week's speaker was the picture of perfection, way too perfect for someone as tired and flawed as I was. I slid further and further down in my seat as the hours in that first week dragged by.

Week two started. Another guest lecturer was speaking to us. To me, it seemed that he was struggling to "catch his stride" and I actually felt a bit of sympathy for him in the first hour or so. He had a much more relaxed style, more of a storyteller than a typical lecturer. He spoke to us for two hours on Monday, two more hours on Tuesday, and then another two hours on Wednesday.

Wednesday's session ended at lunchtime. As we were walking to the outdoor mezzanine where our meals were served, Patti commented on how much she was enjoying the speaker and then asked me what I thought of him. My emotionless response seems as strange now as it did then.

"I don't know. I can't remember anything he said."

Patti let it go.

The next day's activities included another two-hour lecture. Once again, I was sitting in the last row. I think our speaker was about halfway through his presentation when I suddenly burst out sobbing—sobbing out loud! No one else in the room was displaying any perceptible emotion in response to the quiet style of teaching and storytelling we were hearing.

To me, it was as if time stopped and the attention of everyone in the room was drawn to the strange outburst from the middle-aged man at the back of the large classroom. Sobbing is never pleasant. Sobbing publicly is even more distasteful. I fought it from the start. It seemed that immediately my wife's hand was on me—patting my back rapidly as one does in uneasy moments. She whispered assurance to me. "It'll be okay, Honey. It's all right!"

One sentence kept circling through my mind as I struggled to rein in my emotions. "I want to hear my dad say, 'Son, I love you.'" I was fighting these words, trying to keep them from landing.

"That's stupid!" I thought. "I've made it this far without hearing those words. Leave it alone!" I tried to squeeze the words out of my mind. I thought of my dad, thousands of miles away and eighty-two years old at the time. Why trouble him now? He has been a good dad.

Not soon enough, I regained my composure. That night I started to write my father a letter. It took me three weeks to finish it and by the time I mailed it, I knew that this was about something a lot bigger than hearing my dad say, "Son, I love you."

It was about my inability to receive my Heavenly Father's love. It seems that I had built a wall around my heart[1] over years of

---

[1] Bruce Thompson, *Walls of My Heart*

daily living and pastoral ministry. I had built it to keep people from hurting me, to protect myself from careless words, selfish demands and the assorted fickle behavior of humankind. In my thinking, this wall allowed me to filter what I let in and what I kept out. It was my own "wall of salvation."[1]

I was beginning to understand why I couldn't remember anything that our teacher was saying that week. He was telling us stories about the love he as a father had for his children and about God as a father and of the love that He had for His children. In contradiction to his quiet voice and story-telling style, our teacher was swinging a very large sledgehammer. It was hitting the unseen wall that I had built to protect my heart. I couldn't remember anything he said because I was terrified. I knew that if his gentle words kept bashing that wall, it was going to break. And I didn't know what was behind it. What would happen to me if it came crashing down?

By now the damage was done, the wall was coming down, and the healing had begun. In the three weeks it took me to write the letter, I saw new words in the Bible. I saw that God had told His Son that He loved Him, that He brought Him pleasure. It happened when John baptized Jesus. It happened before Jesus had performed one miracle or taught a single lesson to the crowds.

> Jesus was baptized . . . [and] as he was praying, heaven was opened and the Holy Spirit descended on him in bodily form like a dove. And a voice came from heaven: "You are my Son, whom I love; with you I am well pleased."[2]

---

[1] See Isaiah 60:18
[2] Luke 3:21b. 22

On another special occasion, God spoke His love for His Son in the presence of Peter, James, and John on the mountain when He was transfigured as they watched.

> a bright cloud enveloped them, and a voice from the cloud said, "This is my Son, whom I love; with him I am well pleased. Listen to him!"[1]

If God told Jesus that He loved Him, it must be normal for fathers to tell their sons that they love them! Maybe it wasn't stupid after all. Jesus lived with a sense of His Father's pleasure over Him. He wasn't constantly striving to gain His approval. His ministry was not done in an attempt to win His Father's love or acceptance. He was already loved before He taught the multitudes, healed the sick, and fed the hungry. His Father was already pleased with Him before He went to the cross to die for the sins of the world.

By the time I had finished the letter to Dad, I told him that what I really needed was to hear my Heavenly Father speak His love to me. I dropped the letter off at the small post office on campus.

It was weeks later when I heard my name during the afternoon mail call. I stepped forward and took the legal size envelope that was being waved over the expectant crowd. A quick glance at the envelope let me know that it was a letter from Dad. His once streamlined writing style learned in his youth now showed the faltering lines of age. I left the crowd for a place alone.

I opened the envelope. Inside was a full sized sheet of lined paper. I unfolded it and started to read.

---

[1] Matthew 17:5b

Dear son Gaylord,

Thank you for the letter you wrote to let me know how you feel.

I don't know if I ever said "I love You." I should have said it. I am sorry because I didn't. It would have been better for you.

I love you. I wasn't use to hear this when I grew up.

This is poor letter. Correct mistake. Haven't written letter for years

Love

Your dad

I read your letter three times Thank you for it.

I've received a lot of letters in my life. This is the best letter I've ever received. I can't see any mistakes in it. It's perfect!

Dad's simple words taught me one of the most valuable lessons I have ever learned. You cannot give away what you don't have, something you haven't received for yourself.

"I love you. I wasn't use to hear this when I grew up."

My dad never heard these words from his father. And I doubt that his father heard them from his father either. You cannot give away what you don't have.

That was one lesson, but not the biggest. I was beginning to understand that God was my Father. I had known that truth theologically for many years, but now I was starting to experience what I had only grasped intellectually before. God was more than a distant Creator. He was my Father and He loved me deeply. There was no love deficit in Him. He had enough love to go around, enough to fill and overflow every one of us with His love. God is love.[1] He loved me!

I learned that I could trust God enough to let him demolish the walls of protection that I had built around my heart. They were ill-conceived, my own crude attempt to "save myself." The walls I had built were actually keeping me from experiencing my Heavenly Father's love for me, keeping His love from nourishing my thirsty soul—a soul that was designed to hear the words "Son, I love you."

As my trust in Him grew, I accepted the walls of salvation[2] that God had provided for my protection. They were the only walls I needed. I was safe. One by one, the voices of self-condemnation were silenced. I could now receive His words of affirmation. I began to have a growing sense of His pleasure over me as one of His children. I began to experience more of my Heavenly Father's love for me.

For the first time, the words of John the apostle began to have personal meaning to me.

> How great is the love the Father has lavished on us, that we should be called children of God! And that is what we are![3]

Like my dad's "*I wasn't use to hear this when I grew up,*" I wasn't used to thinking of God's love as "lavish." For me, it had been rather carefully measured—as if there was only *so much* of it to go around. I was more accustomed to hearing "Don't take too much. You don't deserve it anyway. And if you do take

---

[1] 1 John 4:16b
[2] Isaiah 60:18
[3] 1 John 3:1a

some, make sure you don't waste any or you might not get any next time I'm giving out love!"

Of course, that thinking affected how I loved others. I couldn't help but be stinted in the way I loved those around me. Besides, I needed to save what love I did have for God.

As I was learning more about the lavish love of our Heavenly Father, my wife and I were in the Philippines for several weeks. A rather large group of us were guests in a compound that had a very limited water supply. Conservation was imperative. Showers were particularly critical. A small soup can, equipped with a crude wire hook, had been hung on the shower faucet. We were restricted to three small soup cans of water per shower. We learned to "make do."

Now, take an imaginary journey with me. Let's pretend that one day the group decided to take a hike into the mountainous forest outside the city. As we are hiking, we begin to hear a low rumble in the distance, almost like a train approaching. It gets louder as we continue up the path. Then we begin to feel a vibration in the ground as we walk. As we come around a bend in the path, we are treated to the amazing spectacle of a huge waterfall cascading down the mountainside!

Someone suggests, "Let's get in. Let's let it shower down over us!"

"But wait," another cautions. "Did anyone bring the soup can?"

That was the way I viewed God's love. Now, I'm learning of His lavish love. A completely new paradigm has been created.

> God has poured out his love into our hearts by the Holy
> Spirit, whom he has given us.[1]

---

[1] Romans 5:5b

If we are going to obey the Command Jesus gave us—to love one another as He loved us—we are going to need an endless supply of love! We will need to be filled with the Holy Spirit continually. Only then can the rivers of His love flow out of us to other thirsty souls.

> Jesus stood and said in a loud voice, 'If anyone is thirsty, let him come to me and drink. Whoever believes in me, as the Scripture has said, streams of living water will flow from within him.' By this he meant the Spirit, whom those who believed in him were later to receive.[1]

We can *discover* Jesus' Commandment by intellectually comprehending what Jesus taught us. That is a very significant step. However, the *recovery* of the Command is dependent upon us receiving the Father's love. We will need to let Jesus show us the Father! And we will need to fully receive and live in the lavish love He has for us as His children.

During our sabbatical, we were separated from our family by thousands of miles for nearly six months. I couldn't help but wonder what it would be like the first time I saw my dad again. Would he say "the words?"

Dad and Mom met us at the airport in San Francisco. It was "Hello" and a hand shake from Dad and big hug from Mom. It was great to see them again and we enjoyed getting caught up on the latest news during the four hour ride back to our home in Chico.

---

[1] John 7:37b-39a

Because we live in the same town, I saw my dad a number of times over the weeks that followed. While I still wanted to hear the words, there was no spoken, "Son, I love you."

Christmas day arrived. We were gathering at Dad and Mom's place to celebrate this special day. Family was trickling in for the meal that would start our time together. As my family and I arrived, I walked into the living room where Dad was in his familiar recliner. As was my habit, I walked toward where he was seated, to shake hands and say "Hello."

But this time he was on his feet, walking toward me. "I have something I want to tell you." Our hands met in a welcoming handshake.

"I love you."

"I love you too, Dad!"

It was a moment I will never forget. That was over fifteen years ago but I'm crying in Starbucks just writing about it . . . napkins piling up all over! It was such a brave moment for Dad and a long awaited one for me. He was able say those words two more times over the months that followed. I'll treasure them forever.

Dad hasn't said them to me for many years now. It would be nice to hear them again but I really don't crave them. I have always known that he loved me and that reality will never change.

Besides, I hear them more often now. While I still have times when fear and doubt try to intrude, I'm getting better at receiving my Heavenly Father's love. I try to start every day with some moments consciously devoted to affirming that life-giving connection. His lavish love is enabling me to grow in personal obedience to Jesus' Command—to love others as He loved me.

When Jesus gave us the New Commandment, He never intended that we would fulfill His Command out of sheer willpower, determination, or self-discipline. He was counting on us receiving the love of God just as He had received His Father's love. Remember Jesus' words.

As the Father has loved me, so have I loved you.[1]

Receiving the Father's love is the bridge that will get us to the place where we were designed to live. His love enables us to "live a life of love."[2] This is what Paul was saying when he wrote that we were to be "imitators of God . . . as dearly loved children and live a life of love, just as Christ loved us . . ."[3]

It is imperative that we know God as more than the Creator. We need to know Him as our Father. To know Him as our Father, we must be "born of Him," born from above by the Spirit and the Word. Jesus said, "Flesh gives birth to flesh, but the Spirit gives birth to spirit. You should not be surprised at my saying, 'You must be born again.'"[4]

We all have a birthday, the day that "flesh gave birth to flesh." On that day, we became the child of our parents. That birth enabled us to experience life as we all know it, to be a member of a family and to see the "kingdoms of this world."

Jesus taught us of another Kingdom, one founded in love by God who is love. He said we could only see and enter that kingdom after we had been born from above—born again. Peter

---

[1] John 15:9a
[2] Ephesians 5:2b
[3] Ephesians 5:1b, 2a
[4] John 3:6-7

writes of this new birth, linking it with the love we have for each other.

> love one another deeply, from the heart. For you have been born again, not of perishable seed, but of imperishable, through the living and enduring word of God.[1]

If you have never experienced this *new birth*, here is a simple prayer that will help you start this amazing journey.

God, Be My Father

God, I believe that You are the Creator. Now I want to know You as my Father. Jesus said, "I am the way and the truth and the life. No one comes to the Father except through Me."

Jesus, I believe in You—all that You said, did, and are for me. I believe that You died for my sin, that You were buried, and that You were raised from death on the third day so I could have the gift of forgiveness and of eternal life. With gratitude, I receive Your gift of forgiveness and of eternal life.

Jesus, I am turning from my ways to Your way. You are my Teacher, Savior, and Lord. I want to learn all You have to teach me about the Father.

Welcome to the family![2]

---

[1] 1 Peter 1:22b, 23

[2] I have several suggestions in Appendix D about how to grow as a follower of Jesus.

CHAPTER 19

CONCLUSION: TOUCHING THE TITANIC

Today, I did something I never dreamed I would do. I touched the Titanic. Actually, it would be more accurate to say I touched a *piece* of the Titanic—a thick triangular iron plate with gnarly rivets embedded in it.[1] It was the only artifact in the Titanic Exhibition that the curious were invited to touch. This chunk of metal had been ripped from the hull by the ship's impact with an iceberg on the fateful night of April 15, 1912.

By morning's light, some two-thirds of the 2,224 people who had so recently and hopefully boarded the ship were no longer in "the land of the living." The unthinkable had happened. On its maiden voyage, the unsinkable Titanic slid out of sight in the frigid waters off Newfoundland.

Seventy-three years later on September 1, 1985, the Titanic was rediscovered. It was embedded in the ocean floor two and a half miles below the surface of the Atlantic. Since that time, there have been numerous deep-sea explorations that have taken amazing pictures of the ship and brought up artifacts for people to view and to touch.

Many important lessons have been learned from this tragic event. We learned that while a journey can begin well, a lack of vigilance could lead to terrible loss. There is another lesson we cannot afford to miss. The Titanic was *rediscovered*, but *not*

---

[1] On April 2, 2007, I went through the Titanic Exhibition at Turtle Bay in Redding, California.

recovered! There is a vast difference between *rediscovery* and *recovery*.

So it is with Jesus' Command. History reveals that this journey started well for the Church. A reading of the book of Acts gives evidence that these first believers loved one another deeply. The letters that follow in the New Testament confirm the vibrant growth of faith in Jesus Christ and love for one another among the first Christians.

In the year 197 A.D., Tertullian, an apologist and leader in the church in North Africa, wrote the following words.

> we have our treasure-chest . . . piety's deposit fund to support and bury poor people, to supply the wants of boys and girls destitute of means and parents, and of old persons confined now to the house; such, too, as have suffered shipwreck; and if there happen to be any in the mines, or banished to the islands, or shut up in the prisons, for nothing but their fidelity to the cause of God's Church, *It is mainly the deeds of love so noble that lead many to put a brand upon us. They say, "See how they love one another!"*[1]

With such a vibrant start, one could question whether it is even possible to lose Jesus' Command. Nevertheless, Jesus warned His disciples of a time when "many will turn away from the faith . . . and hate each other"[2] and "the love of most will grow cold."[3] In His final instructions, Jesus implies that His Command could be lost when He used the word *tereo*, "teaching

---

[1] Tertullian, *Tertullian's Apology* (197 A.D.), Chapter 39, AGES, p. 84
[2] Matthew 24:10b
[3] Matthew 24:12b

them *to guard*—to protect by never taking your eyes off[1]—everything I have commanded you."[2]

I didn't have to look beyond the record of Scripture to see the necessity of guarding this precious Command and the possibility of its loss. Consider the young church in Ephesus. Early on, Paul was clearly encouraged by the *faith* and *love* that characterized the believers there. He wrote, "ever since I heard about your faith in the Lord Jesus and your love for all the saints, I have not stopped giving thanks for you, remembering you in my prayers."[3] It was an excellent start.

But when John wrote to them thirty years later, he mixes his commendation with an impassioned warning.

> You have forsaken your first love. Remember the height from which you have fallen! Repent and do the things you did at first. If you do not repent, I will come to you and remove your lampstand from its place.[4]

While the Ephesian church had many admirable qualities, John pointed out their failure to guard Jesus' Command. They did not love one another as they had at first. Their mark of authenticity had been lost. It was imperative that they repent. As a follow-up to this warning, it is believed by many that John spent the last years of his long life in Ephesus and reminded them often of the Lord's Command.

I know that for me, Jesus' Command was lost! When I saw the Command on May 1, 2002, I assumed that I was the only one that had missed this amazingly significant declaration. Immediately, I had turned to Bercot's dictionary to learn more

---

[1] From my comment on Matthew 28:20
[2] Matthew 28:20a
[3] Ephesians 1:15b-16
[4] Revelation 2:4b-5

about my discovery from the early fathers. I was stunned when I found no reference to it among the seven hundred topics listed.

This led me to start my own search through the writings of the early church fathers. I needed to find out what had happened to the Command Jesus gave us. In the five years that followed, I spent thousands of hours in search of the answer to the question, "What ever happened to Jesus' Command?"[1]

Astonishingly, I found that the loss happened early. While I came across some hopeful moments of *rediscovery* in church history, I have yet to find a point of *recovery*, a time when His Command is broadly given its rightful place in Christian theology and practice.

This is not to say that there have been no pockets of awareness and practice of the Command throughout our long history. Neither am I saying that those pockets of obedience do not exist in the present. On the contrary, I am certain they have always existed and continue in this moment in many unpublished places.

This loss did not mean that the words Jesus spoke in giving His Command have been lost from Scripture. They were always in my Bible even though I did not see them clearly. Rather, the loss has been like a fog that settled over the Commandment, specifically as Jesus gave it, and over the authority with which only He could plant it by His Command within Christian thought and practice.

My personal experience has reminded me that it's possible for something to be right in front of us and not see it. The longest sermon series in my pastoral ministry was given over twenty-five years ago. The series was on "Love" and lasted one year. Yet, I didn't clearly see the Command Jesus gave us.

---

[1] See Appendix 1

I should have been aware of this loss much earlier in my life. Nearly three decades ago, I was stepping into my first senior pastorate. I had served that congregation as a youth pastor and associate pastor. It had grown significantly during that decade and now, with the retirement of the founding pastor, I was being asked to assume the lead role.

This change in leadership required the governing body of the congregation to examine the constitution and bylaws that guided this transition. These legal documents contained our statement of purpose, core beliefs, and polity—the rules by which we were governed. What had been adequate for a small congregation seemed inadequate for a larger one. It was unanimously agreed that they needed to be updated.

A search was initiated. In addition to our own denominational affiliation, we contacted over a dozen leading congregations from various Christian persuasions, asking each of them for a copy of their constitution and bylaws.

Having received them, we set aside a room to process the dozen examples we had received. We made copies of each and then cut them into pieces based on common themes and compiled them in stacks. Themes included statement of faith, purpose, polity, and organization to name a few.

Even now, I have a clear picture in my mind of a very significant moment from that assignment. I am standing in the middle of the room holding the stack of statements of faith—core beliefs of each church. I distinctly remember turning to look at another leader in the room and saying these words:

"Does it seem strange to you that none of these mention *loving one another?*"

That was nearly three decades ago. I now know that a majority of Christian denominations make no direct reference to the One Command Jesus gave us—love one another as I have loved you—in their statements of faith and practice.

We are all tempted to say, "But it's in our Bible and we believe it all! The Bible is our statement of faith and practice."

I agree. Yet, in the surveys I've done over the last several years, I find an amazingly consistent response when asking the question, "What is Jesus' Command?" Only one in ten people who embrace the Christian faith include "to love one another" in their answer. (In my last survey of fourteen students in training for Christian service, none included *loving one another* in their brief written answer.)

Obviously, my surveys do not qualify as scientific. However, they are an indicator of a historical reality, one that continues to this very moment. The Command Jesus gave us was lost somewhere in our journey. His Command is still waiting to be *discovered* by our generation.

At this time, it is important to remember several points. First, the subject of this book is very narrow, yet very important— *rediscovering* the lost Command of Jesus. I am not addressing broad areas of theology or church history. Without apology, my focus is the One Command Jesus gave us.

Second, we should never turn this information into criticism of historical figures, the church, or Christianity in general. Rather, I urge each of us to *own* church history. It is "our history." Its strengths and victories are ours. So also are its weaknesses and failures. Our response should be one of sorrow for our historic failure to guard Jesus' Command. This should bring us to humble ourselves, to pray and turn from both our personal and historic neglect of the command to love one another as Jesus loved us. This repentance will make way for forgiveness, reconciliation, and healing of the deep wounds created by our disobedience.

Third, hindsight is always 20/20! We have never faced the challenges that were faced by our fathers in the faith. It is impossible for us to fully appreciate the difficulties that they had to overcome in their day. Any progress we make must be carried in humility.

Fourth, we must live in the present. We are making church history in this very moment. Our criticism of the past will change nothing. Yet if we fail to learn from history, we will repeat the mistakes of our past. Our constructive response in discovering, recovering, and guarding Jesus' Command will be significant in the history that is being written through our lives.

Finally, remember that this is not about choosing between faith in Jesus Christ or love for one another. It is both of them together! It is the New Covenant and the New Commandment—inextricably linked.

Personal Discovery

Discovery is personal. It is one person at a time. I have shared some of my personal journey of discovery with you. I trust that you have started that joyful journey as well. I want you to live the rest of your life as a believer who deeply trusts in Jesus and as one who will "guard—to protect by never taking your eyes off—" the Command He gave us.

That will lead you on the personal adventure of *recovering* His Command. You will be part of a *love revolution*—one that takes us full-circle, back to the feet of Jesus who is "the author and finisher of our faith."[1]

There is another way you play a strategic role. You have a sphere of influence. I'm asking you to pass this message on to those you encounter in life. As you share the Good News about *faith in Jesus Christ* and His Command to *love one another*, the *discovery* of Jesus' Command can spread to family, friends, and associates.

Church Rediscovery

There is another facet to this *love revolution—rediscovery*. *Rediscovery* is for the church. For there to be a broad *recovery* of the Command, the church must *rediscover* the Command it held in the beginning. The process of *rediscovery* may begin with a pastor, congregational leaders, or a small group. Then it can spread to an entire congregation. New believer and membership classes can include training which deliberately includes Jesus' Commandment.

All branches of the Christian church can place Jesus' Command prominently in their catechisms and statements of faith and practice. Missionary organizations and discipleship movements can *rediscover* the Command and incorporate it into their training models.

For this *love revolution* to succeed, Christian theologies must incorporate Jesus' Command into their systems. For *rediscovery* to occur, seminaries and schools of Biblical studies will need to feature the Command in their course of study.

---

[1] Hebrews 12:2b KJV

Recovery

Rediscovery is significant—very significant in my thinking, but rediscovery is not *recovery*. Rediscovering Jesus' Commandment enables us to examine its original splendor. We can begin to imagine what it would have been like if His Command had been a centerpiece of Christianity for all these years. We can think through the tragic effects of its loss in both church and world history. We can postulate about what contributed to the catastrophic loss. However, none of that is *recovering* the Command.

We must go beyond personal *discovery* and church *rediscovery*. Jesus' Command must not simply become a museum piece for curious fingers to touch. Rather, it must be fully restored to its place as a *core commandment* of authentic Christianity. That is when *discovery* and *rediscovery* become *recovery*, all of us embracing once again the Command that was held so poignantly in the beginning.

The *recovery* of His Command is directly related to the prayer that Jesus prayed to the Father.

> *I ask that those who will believe in me through their message may all be one, as you, Father, are in me and I in you. I ask that they also may be one in us—brought to complete unity that the world may believe and know that you sent me and have loved them as you loved me.*[1]

I am persuaded that the Father will answer the prayer of His Son! I believe that those who embrace the core commands of Christianity will be a living testament, one written in answer to that prayer.

---

[1] My paraphrase of John 17:20-23

And this is his [God's] command: to believe in the name of his Son, Jesus Christ, and to love one another as he [Jesus] commanded us.[1]

We know that we have passed from death to life, because we love our brothers.[2]

By this all men will know that you are my disciples, if you love one another.[3]

Here is a prayer I invite you to pray with me.

Fill Me with Your Love

God, thank You for being my Father and for Your lavish love for me. Thank You for showing me Your love through Your Son, Jesus Christ.

I want to be filled with Your love. Pour Your love into me by the Holy Spirit. Fill me so full of Your love that it becomes a stream, a river that overflows and refreshes me and everyone I encounter in life.

I want to guard the Command Jesus gave me—to love one another. Empowered by Your Holy Spirit, teach me how to live a life of love and be a true disciple and a worshipper of God!

Thanks for being part of a *love revolution*!

---

[1] 1 John 3:23
[2] 1 John 3:14a
[3] John 13:35

AN INVITATION FROM THE AUTHOR . . .

I am encouraging a *love revolution*—a growing movement of believers that are committed to (1) faith in Jesus Christ and (2) love for one another. With this in mind, I am urging Christians everywhere to pray for the coming of God's Kingdom, agreeing that His will be done on earth as it is in Heaven. I am certain this includes the full *recovery* of Jesus' Command.

I am not a person who can afford to be presumptuous or arrogant. I've been to "the edge" a number of times. I live with a sense of dependence on God's grace, protection, and sustaining love. This dependence is expressed in the words of James.

> *Now listen, you who say, "Today or tomorrow we will go to this or that city, spend a year there, carry on business and make money." Why, you do not even know what will happen tomorrow. What is your life? You are a mist that appears for a little while and then vanishes. Instead, you ought to say, "If it is the Lord's will, we will live and do this or that."*[1]

If it is the Lord's will, I plan to continue writing on this theme with a focus on *recovering* Jesus' Command. I am interested in

---

[1] James 4:13-15

receiving short accounts of your personal experience in *discovering* and *recovering* Jesus' Command and living a life of love.

If your congregation, denomination, or educational institution is taking action steps to *recover* Jesus' Command, I would like receive an outline of those steps and hear a short account of your progress.

Please send them to:

E-mail: mystory@jesuscommand.com

My Story
PO Box 6790
Chico, CA 95927

I look forward to learning together.

Love and Blessings,
Gaylord Enns

CHAPTER DISCUSSION QUESTIONS

Prologue: A Day Gone Awry

"And we know that in all things God works for the good of those who love him, who have been called according to his purpose." Romans 8:28

1. Have you experienced a major life-altering crisis? (If not you, what about someone very close to you?)

2. How did it impact your life?

3. In what ways have you seen God at work to bring some good out of the difficulty?

4. How can you apply Romans 8:28 to your life?

Chapter 1 - An Empty Table

"make disciples of all the nations, baptizing them in the name of the Father and the Son and the Holy Spirit. Teach these new disciples to obey all the commands I have given you." Matthew 28:19b-20a (New Living Translation)

1. What events surround the occasion on which Jesus speaks these words?

2. What proclamation does Jesus make before commissioning them to "make disciples?"

3. What does the author identify as Jesus' embedded definition of disciple making?

4. How can you apply this in your life?

Chapter 2 - All That I Commanded

"A new command I give you: Love one another. As I have loved you, so you must love one another. By this all men will know that you are my disciples, if you love one another." John 13:34-35

1. On what occasion does Jesus introduce this New Command?

2. When asked the question, "What is Jesus' Command," what has your answer been?

3. Why would we call this Jesus' Commandment?

4. How can you apply this in your life?

Chapter 3 - The Early Fathers

"Then Jesus came to them and said, 'All authority in heaven and on earth has been given to me. Therefore go and make disciples of all nations . . . teaching them to obey everything I commanded you.'" Matthew 28:18, 19a, 20a

1. Whom does the author identify as the "early fathers?"

2. What is the deeper meaning of "obey?"

3. What are we instructed to guard?

4. How can you apply this in your life?

Chapter 4 - Core Commandments

"And this is his command: to believe in the name of his Son, Jesus Christ, and to love one another as he commanded us." 1 John 3:23

1. When we read "And this is his command," to whom is John referring?

2. When we read "as he commanded us," to whom is John referring?

3. Why does the author call these the "core commandments of Christianity?"

4. How can you apply this in your life?

Chapter 5 - You Can Ask A Question

"The King will reply, 'I tell you the truth, whatever you did for one of the least of these brothers of mine, you did for me.'" Matthew 25:40

1. What question was troubling the author? Can you identify with his question?

2. Who is the "King" in this account?

3. Where is "God's new home" and why is this important?

4. How can you apply this in your life?

Chapter 6 - A Breakfast Surprise

"If someone says, 'I love God,' but hates a Christian brother or sister, that person is a liar; for if we don't love people we can see, how can we love God, whom we have not seen?" 1 John 4:20 New Living Translation

1. Why is it impossible to love God if one does not love his Christian brothers and sisters?

2. Why does the author say that when we love one another, we give God a "double hug?"

3. Does Jesus ever come to your house?

4. How can you apply this in your life?

Chapter 7 - Comparing the Old and New

"This is real love. It is not that we loved God, but that he loved us and sent his Son as a sacrifice to take away our sins. Dear friends, since God loved us that much, we surely ought to love each other." 1 John 4:10-11 New Living Translation

1. What does the author identify as the core commandments of the Old Testament?

2. What does the author identify as the core commandments of the New Testament?

3. What is the most significant difference between the two?

4. How can you apply this in your life?

Chapter 8 - The Time Is Coming

"'The time is coming,' declares the LORD, 'when I will make a new covenant with the house of Israel and with the house of Judah.'" Jeremiah 31:31

1. What covenant existed at the time Jeremiah spoke these words? Discuss the "when, where and who" of both the existing and promised covenants.

2. Why was a new covenant needed?

3. How did God prepare them for this change?

4. How can you apply this in your life?

Chapter 9 - *NOT Like the Covenant*

"'It will not be like the covenant I made with their forefathers when I took them by the hand to lead them out of Egypt, because they broke my covenant . . .' declares the LORD." Jeremiah 31:32a, c

1. Why were the words "not be like" important to the people Jeremiah was speaking to?

2. Why are those words important to us today?

3. What change stands out to you as being most significant?

4. How can you apply this in your life?

Chapter 10 - JESUS!

When all the people were being baptized, Jesus was baptized too. And as he was praying, heaven was opened and the Holy Spirit descended on him in bodily form like a dove. And a voice came from heaven: "You are my Son, whom I love; with you I am well pleased." Luke 3:21-22

1. What can we learn about God from Luke 3:21-22?

2. What can we learn about Jesus from the words of John who baptized Jesus? (Is this the same John who became a disciple of Jesus?)

3. What is the significance of the phrase "the Lamb of God?"

4. How can you apply this in your life?

Chapter 11 - New Covenant, New Commandment

"And he [Jesus] took bread, gave thanks and broke it, and gave it to them, saying, 'This is my body given for you; do this in remembrance of me.' In the same way, after the supper he took the cup, saying, 'This cup is the new covenant in my blood, which is poured out for you.'" Luke 22:19-20

1. Why are the words "New Covenant" so significant to us?

2. What kind of leadership would you say Jesus modeled?

3. What is the significance of announcing the New Covenant and the New Commandment on the same night?

4. How can you apply this in your life?

Chapter 12 - One New Person

"His purpose was to make peace between Jews and Gentiles by creating in himself one new person from the two groups. Together as one body, Christ reconciled both groups to God by means of his death [on the cross]" Ephesians 2:15b-16a New Living Translation

1. Why had the two ethnicities (Jews and Gentiles) been divided historically?

2. What metaphor did Jesus use to tell His followers that the division between Jews and Gentiles would be abolished?

3. Why would the New Commandment be significant to each ethnicity in the New Covenant?

4. How can you apply this in your life?

Chapter 13 - Love One Another!

"Dear friends, let us love one another, for love comes from God. Everyone who loves has been born of God and knows God. Whoever does not love does not know God, because God is love." 1 John 4:7-8

1. Why does the author believe Jesus' Command is so important to understanding the New Testament letters?

2. Is it possible that Jesus' Commandment was lost early in Christian history?

3. What correlation is there between church history and the loss of Jesus' Command? What about world history?

4. How can you apply this in your life?

Chapter 14 - The King's Law

"But if you keep looking steadily into God's perfect law - the law that sets you free - and if you do what it says and don't forget what you heard, then God will bless you for doing it." James 1:25 New Living Translation

1. What is unique about James and the position he filled?

2. Why was "love your neighbor as yourself" used by James to define the King's Law?

3. What connection is there between "the perfect law" and "freedom?"

4. How can you apply this in your life?

Chapter 15 - The Law of Christ

"Carry each other's burdens, and in this way you will fulfill the law of Christ." Galatians 6:2

1. What connection do you see between the Law of Christ and Jesus' Command?

2. What do you see as the difference between being "under the Law of Moses" and being "in the Law of Christ?"

3. How could the entire Law be summed up in a single command?

4. How can you apply this in your life?

Chapter 16 - Love Covers—Love Confronts

"Above all, love each other deeply, because love covers over a multitude of sins." 1 Peter 4:8

1. What makes Peter's words about loving one another unique?

2. What is the difference between "love that covers" and "a cover-up?"

3. What does Jesus' confrontation with Peter teach us?

4. How can you apply this in your life?

Chapter 17 - Do I Love 'em or Hate 'em?

"If anyone says, 'I am living in the light,' but hates a Christian brother or sister, that person is still living in darkness. Anyone who loves other Christians is living in the light and does not cause anyone to stumble." 1 John 2:9-10 New Living Translation

1. Why is there no "mushy-middle-ground" between love and hate in the Bible?

2. What does indifference look like? What does concern look like?

3. What correlation do you see between Jesus' Command and unity among Christians?

4. How can you apply this in your life?

Chapter 18 - Bridge: Words I Want To Hear

"How great is the love the Father has lavished on us, that we should be called children of God! And that is what we are!" 1 John 3:1

1. What kept the author from experiencing God's love?

2. What connection is there between receiving the Father's love and loving one another as Jesus commanded?

3. How do we actually receive and experience God's love?

4. How can you apply this in your life?

Chapter 19 - Conclusion: Touching the Titanic

"But I have this complaint against you. You don't love me or each other as you did at first! Look how far you have fallen from your first love! Turn back . . ." Revelation 2:4-5a New Living Translation

1. Can you relate to the author's personal discovery of Jesus' Command?

2. In your experience, is there a need for Christians in general to discover Jesus' Command?

3. How do you understand the author's use of the words *discover*, *rediscover,* and *recover*?

4. Will you be part of a *love revolution*?

APPENDICES

Commands vs. Command in the New Testament

I had a question about Jesus' interchangeable use of the words *commands* (plural) and *command* (singular). Is Jesus talking about one command or many commands? (See John 14:15, 21; 15:10, 12). John also uses the alternating singular and plural in writing his letters (See 1 John 2:3-8; 3:21-24; 5:2-3; 1 John 1:6).

Here is the best answer I have come across. Kettel's *Theological Dictionary of the New Testament* and provides this explanation for the mixture of the singular and plural in these cases.

> "the plural 'commands' . . . is simply a development of John's favourite concept of unity" "The [use of the plural] 'commands' always summed up in the one command of love, do not imply a Jewish multiplicity of ordinances, but the radiating of the one 'command' out into the manifoldness of the obedient life." "It is (the) . . . fulfilment of the commandments as the one commandment grounded in Jesus."

Kettel's *Theological Dictionary of the New Testament.* Copyright © 1964 By Wm. B. Eerdmans Publishing Co., pp. 554

APPENDIX B

Uses of "command" (entellomai or entole) in the Gospels

The word *command* (*entellomai* or *entole*) is found in all four of the Gospel accounts. It is important to recognize that this word differs from the more frequent use of the *aorist imperative* in Greek language that also indicates an authoritative thrust in what is spoken.

Gospel according to Matthew: Matthew uses the word command (entellomai and entole) twelve times. Of the twelve, Jesus applied it universally as His command in one unique instance.

> Matthew 28:20 "and teaching them to obey everything *I have commanded* you. And surely I am with you always, to the very end of the age."

Gospel according to Mark: Of the ten times the word *command* (*entellomai* and *entole*) is used by Mark, there is no unique instance in which Jesus applied it universally as His command.

Gospel according to Luke: Of the five times the word *command* (*entellomai* and *entole*) is used by Luke, there is no unique instance in which Jesus applied it universally as His command.

Gospel according to John: John uses the word command (entellomai and entole) fourteen times in his account of the Gospel. Of the fourteen times, Jesus applied it universally as His command in seven unique instances.

John 13:34 "A new **command I give** you: Love one another. As I have loved you, so you must love one another."

John 14:15 "If you love me, you will obey what **I command**."

John 14:21 "Whoever has **my commands** and obeys them, he is the one who loves me. He who loves me will be loved by my Father, and I too will love him and show myself to him."

John 15:10 "If you obey **my commands**, you will remain in my love, just as I have obeyed my Father's commands and remain in his love."

John 15:12 "**My command** is this: Love each other as I have loved you."

John 15:14 "You are my friends if you do what **I command**."

John 15:17 "This is **my command**: Love each other."

APPENDIX C

Jesus' Command in the Writings of the Early Fathers (125-325 A.D.)

In the years that followed my original search in Bercot's work, I did my own search of the writings of the ante Nicene fathers and found six direct references to Jesus' Command. One was in the writings of Clement of Alexandria from the end of the second century. Four were in the writings of Cyprian, bishop of Carthage from about the middle of the third century. I found one direct reference in *Apostolic Teaching and Constitution*, a compiled document that was in existence at the end of the third century.

Additionally, there are numerous references to *loving one another* without direct reference to the Command having been given to us by Jesus as the New Command or His Command.

Appendix D

Growing as a Follower of Jesus

I would highlight three areas for you as you start this new life.

1. Reading the New Testament Scriptures

Based on my own personal experience, I would encourage you to start by reading John's Gospel (the fourth book in the New Testament). I recommend reading through it as you would read a letter you have just opened from a friend. (This may take a few days.) Then start over at the beginning and read for more detail, focusing on points you missed the first time. I recommend highlighting some parts of the text that seem to stand out as very significant for you at this time. Finally, read it a third time. Look for more details as you go through. Select several sentences (verses) that really seem significant for you and memorize them. (Also, memorize the number of the chapter and verse so you can find them easily.)

Following John, I would suggest reading Acts. This is the book that follows John's Gospel. This will give you a picture of what life as a follower of Jesus looked like in the beginning. It will also give you a sequence of events in the first thirty years of Christianity.

I would then suggest John's letters near the end of the New Testament. There are three of them and they are very short. (Again, I recommend following the "three-reading" approach I suggested earlier.)

Following that, I would recommend reading Paul's letter to the Ephesians, then Peter's two letters followed by the letter written by James. Start to intersperse the Gospels according to Mark, Matthew, and Luke.

I would suggest that you spend the first year reading in the New Testament. My reasoning is simple: it is the New Covenant, the one that relates directly to you and provides a clear and relevant foundation for your understanding of the Christian faith.

2. Prayer

Prayer is simply communication with God. It is talking to Him and listening as well. The prayer Jesus taught us to pray is a wonderful pattern of prayer. You will find it in Matthew 5:9-15.

You will see many examples of prayer as you read the New Testament. Use these prayers as models as you come across them.

Finally, follow your heart in prayer. Express your thoughts and feelings toward God. As you would with a loving "earthly" father, ask your heavenly Father for wisdom on decisions in life and for His help in daily living.

3. Being Together With Other Followers of Jesus

It is normal for family to be together. You will notice how this happened as you read Acts. Early Christians got together in big gatherings and in small groups. I would recommend that you adopt this as a pattern for your life.

In our western culture, the large gatherings usually happen in a church building. Some of the buildings are very large and others are quite small. Some look like a church building and others don't. As part of your prayers to God, ask Him to guide you to a "church family" that will encourage you in your life of faith in Jesus Christ and remind you to guard Jesus' Command to love one another as He loves you.

APPENDIX E

Bible Translations

(KJV) *King James Version*

(NAS) *New American Standard Bible.* Anaheim: Foundation Press, 1973

(NKJV) *New King James Version.* Nashville: Thomas Nelson, 1982

(NLT) *New Living Translation.* Wheaton: Tyndale, 1996, 2004

(YLT) *Young's Literal Translation of the Old and New Testaments.* Robert Young, 1898

Aramaic New Testament - Khabouris Codex.
Cover: Our thanks to Dr. Michael Ryce for permission to use an image of page 237 of his Khaburis/Khaboris web site at http://whyagain.com/KhaburisKhaboris/. This page contains an image of the ancient Aramaic text we know as John 13:34-35. The text shown was written around 1050 A.D. It is believed to have been copied from Aramaic Scripture written as early as the second century.

BIBLIOGRAPHY

Augustine. *Enchiridion-On Faith, and Love.* Translated and edited by
Albert C. Outler. Albany: AGES Digital Library, 1967.

Bercot, David W. *A Dictionary of Early Christian Beliefs.* Peabody:
Hendrickson, 1998.

Brown, Colin, ed. *Dictionary of New Testament Theology.* Grand Rapids:
Zondervan, 1986.

Calvin, John. *Institutes of the Christian Religion.* Edited by John T.
McNeill. Philadelphia: Westminster, 1967.

————. *The Works of John Calvin* (Calvin's Bible Commentaries,
Calvin's Institutes, General Writings, Sermons). Albany: AGES
Digital Library, 2000.

Chapman, Gary D. *The Five Love Languages.* Chicago: Northfield, 1992.

Clarke, Adam. *Clarke's Commentary, 8 Volumes.* Albany: AGES Digital
Library, 1997.

d'Aubigne, J.H. Merle. *History of the Reformation in Europe in the Time
of Calvin, 4 Volumes.* Albany: AGES Digital Library, 1998.

Denck, Hans. *Selected Writings of Hans Denck.* Edited by E. J. Furcha.
Lewiston: Edwin Mellen Press, 1989.

Encyclopedia Britannica. Chicago: Encyclopedia Britannica, Inc., 2001.

Friedmann, Robert. *The Theology of Anabaptism.* Scottdale: Herald
Press, 1972.

Gonzalez, Justo L. *The Story of Christianity.* New York: Harper Collins,
1984.

Grebel, Konrad. *The Sources of Swiss Anabaptism.* Edited by Leland
Harder. In *Classics of the Radical Reformation.* Edited by
Cornelius J. Dyck. Scottdale: Herald Press, 1985.

Hubmaier, Balthasar. *Classics of the Radical Reformation.* Edited by
    Wayne Pipkin and John H. Yoder. Scottdale: Herald Press, 1989.

Joris, David. *The Anabaptist Writings of David Joris.* Translated and
    edited by Gary K. Waite. Waterloo: Herald Press, 1994.

Kittel, Gerhard. *Theological Dictionary of the New Testament.* Grand
    Rapids: Eerdmans, 1965.

Krahn, Cornelius, ed. *The Mennonite Encyclopedia.* Scottdale:
    Mennonite Publishing House, 1957.

Luther, Martin. *Good Works, Preface To Romans, Table Talk, 95 Theses,
    The Large Catechism, The Small Catechism, The Smalcald
    Articles.* Albany: AGES Digital Library, 2000.

———. *The Martin Luther Collection. 95 Theses, A Commentary on St.
    Paul's Epistle to the Galatians, Luther's Commentary on the
    Sermon on the Mount, The Letters of Martin Luther, Watchwords
    for the Warfare of Life, Prophecies of Luther. Sermons of Luther
    (8 vols.), Works of Luther (6 vols.).* Albany: AGES Digital
    Library, 1998.

Marpeck, Pilgram. *The Writings of Pilgram Marpeck.* In *Classics of the
    Radical Reformation.* Translated and edited by William Klassen
    and Walter Klaassen. Kitchener: Herald Press, 1978.

Melanchthon, Philipp. *The Augsburg Confession.* Albany: AGES Digital
    Library, 1997.

Merriam Webster's Collegiate Dictionary, Tenth Edition. Chicago:
    Merriam Webster, Inc., 2000.

Random House Webster's Unabridged Dictionary. Content Copyright
    1999, 1997, 1996, 1994, 1993, 1987, Software Copyright 1997,
    1996, 1994, 1993 by Lernaut & Haupie.

Roberts, A. and J. Donaldson, eds. *The Ante-Nicene Fathers, 10
    Volumes.* Albany: AGES Digital Library, 1997.

Schaff, Philip, ed. *The Nicene and Post-Nicene Fathers, Series 1, 14 Volumes*. Albany: AGES Digital Library, 1997.

――― . *The Nicene and Post-Nicene Fathers, Series 2, 14 Volumes*. Albany: AGES Digital Library: 1997.

――― . *The History of the Christian Church*. Albany: AGES Digital Library, 1997.

Simons, Menno. *The Complete Writings of Menno Simons*. Translated by Leonard Verduin. Edited by J. C. Wenger. Scottdale: Herald Press, 1956.

Strong, James. *The New Strong's Exhaustive Concordance of the Bible*. New York: Nelson, 1984.

The Ultimate Christian Library. Rio: AGES Digital Library, 2000.

Thompson, Bruce. *Walls of My Heart*. Euclid: Crown, 1989

Wesley, John. *The Works of John Wesley, Third Edition Complete and Unabridged*. 1872.

Wesley, John. *The Works of John Wesley, 14 vols*. Peabody: Hendrickson, 1984.

Young, Robert. *Analytical Concordance to the Bible*. Grand Rapids: Eerdmans, 1971.

Contact Information

Gaylord Enns
Servant Leadership Network
PO Box 6790
Chico, CA 95927-6790

gaylord@servantleadershipnetwork.org

www.servantleadershipnetwork.org

My Story
PO Box 6790
Chico, CA 95927-6790

mystory@jesuscommand.com